AMERICAN HORTICULTURAL SOCIETY
PRACTICAL GUIDES

CLEMATIS

AMERICAN HORTICULTURAL SOCIETY
PRACTICAL GUIDES

CLEMATIS

CHARLES CHESSHIRE

DK PUBLISHING, INC.
www.dk.com

UÉ PH **DK** HT PR PH ~~JW~~ VK

A DK PUBLISHING BOOK
www.dk.com

PROJECT EDITOR Samantha Gray
ART EDITOR Rachael Parfitt

SERIES EDITOR Pamela Brown
SERIES ART EDITOR Stephen Josland
US EDITOR Ray Rogers

MANAGING EDITOR Louise Abbott
MANAGING ART EDITOR Lee Griffiths

DTP DESIGNER Matthew Greenfield

PRODUCTION MANAGER Patricia Harrington

First American Edition, 1999
2 4 6 8 10 9 7 5 3 1

Published in the United States by
DK Publishing, Inc., 95 Madison Avenue, New York, New York 10016

Library of Congress Cataloging-in-Publication Data

Clematis. -- 1st American ed.
    p.   cm. -- (AHS practical guides)
Includes index.
ISBN 0–7894–4153–5 (alk. paper)
1. Clematis.
I. DK Publishing, Inc. II. Series.
SB413.C6C58 1999
635.9'3334--dc21   98–41494
                                    CIP

Reproduced by Colourpath, London
Printed and bound by Star Standard Industries, Singapore

CONTENTS

USING CLEMATIS IN THE GARDEN 7

An introduction to the many ways in which
clematis can be grown in the garden, and how to
choose which sort to put where.

THE CLEMATIS YEAR   10
THE COLOR RANGE   12
PLANNING COLOR COMBINATIONS   14
COMBINING CLEMATIS WITH ROSES   16
CLEMATIS IN THE BORDER   18
CHOOSING HOST TREES AND SHRUBS   20
COVERING VERTICAL SURFACES   22
GROWING CLEMATIS IN CONTAINERS   24

CARING FOR YOUR CLEMATIS 27

Choosing, planting, and training clematis, how
and when to prune the different types, and the best
methods for propagating your own plants.

A GALLERY OF CLEMATIS 49

A photographic guide to the exciting range available,
with the types arranged in order of flowering time.

Index   70
Acknowledgments   72

USING CLEMATIS IN THE GARDEN

WHICH CLEMATIS WHERE?

CLEMATIS ARE SO VERSATILE that even in the smallest garden there are many more possibilities for growing them than most of us realize. With the huge range of species and more than 400 cultivars to choose from, deciding which to grow is both exciting and a bit bewildering. Pick the right one, and it will climb to the treetops or live happily in a pot. It is this versatility, combined with the great variety in flower shape and color, that makes clematis so popular.

TYPES OF FLOWER

Flower shapes range from the gentle, nodding blooms of many of the species clematis to the big, bold showstoppers found among the large-flowered hybrids. As a very rough guide, clematis can be divided into these two major groupings.

With blooms that measure up to 8in/20cm across, it is the large-flowered hybrids that have been bred to put on a dazzling display through summer. The flowers are usually single, but there are also several doubles. The clematis usually referred to as species clematis tend to have smaller flowers of more varied shape that appear in spring, late summer, and autumn. They include, among others, *Clematis armandii*, *C. alpina*, *C. macropetala*, *C. montana*, *C. terniflora*, *C. texensis*, *C. viticella*, *C. tibetana*, and *C. tangutica*. A photographic gallery (*see p.49*) illustrates the range and gives their flowering times.

THE VARIETY OF FLOWER SHAPES

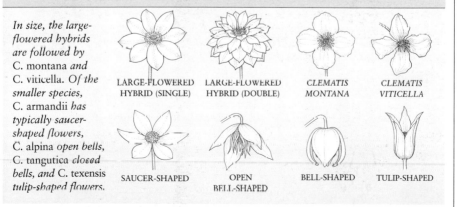

In size, the large-flowered hybrids are followed by C. montana *and* C. viticella. *Of the smaller species,* C. armandii *has typically saucer-shaped flowers,* C. alpina *open bells,* C. tangutica *closed bells, and* C. texensis *tulip-shaped flowers.*

LARGE-FLOWERED HYBRID (SINGLE)   LARGE-FLOWERED HYBRID (DOUBLE)   CLEMATIS MONTANA   CLEMATIS VITICELLA

SAUCER-SHAPED   OPEN BELL-SHAPED   BELL-SHAPED   TULIP-SHAPED

◄ PINK PARTNERS *The large-flowered hybrid 'Comtesse de Bouchaud' with the rose 'Pink Bells'.*

FAMILY ORIGINS

Initially, plant breeders concentrated on the large-flowered hybrids. George Jackman, a nurseryman, produced 'Jackmanii', one of the first and still one of the most popular, in 1862. Since then, hybridizers around the world have been busy extending the range and in recent years have turned their attention to the species, introducing many splendid new plants.

Clematis belong to the same plant family as buttercups, peonies, and anemones. There are over 200 species distributed around the world, but the majority hail from the temperate regions of the northern hemisphere. The eye-catching flowers are not actually composed of petals but of sepals. Typically, a flower has two layers surrounding the stamens – the green sepals that protect the inner parts, and colored petals that attract insects. In a few plants, however, such as clematis, it is the sepals that are colored, looking just like petals.

HOW THEY GROW

The majority of clematis are climbers, and, for the most part, that is why we prize them, growing them up trellises and

▲ OVER THE GATE
'Perle d'Azur' makes a welcoming arch. It is one of the finest of the large-flowered hybrids that bloom in summer.

◄ SWAGS OF RED
'Kermesina' puts on a magnificent show from late summer to autumn. This is a good clematis to grow among shrubs.

pergolas, or around arches and gateways. But it is, above all, their natural ability to grow through and with other plants that makes clematis invaluable. In the wild, they use other plants for support, scrambling through trees and shrubs by twisting their leaf stalks around the twigs. They are often at their best seen growing in this way, and it is an ideal method to adopt in the garden. Clematis can also be used to hide ugly buildings or as a groundcover. They can be planted in pots on a patio, and, in addition, there are several truly herbaceous clematis, excellent for borders and beds.

THROUGH THE SEASONS

By selecting from the many species and hybrids it is possible to have a long succession of different clematis flowers. Some produce fluffy seedheads, like those on *C. terniflora*, the sweet autumn clematis. Those that follow the autumn flowers of *C. tibetana*, *C. tangutica*, and 'Bill MacKenzie' extend the season even

further. The clematis palette includes every color except bright orange. Fragrance is elusive in all but a few of the species, and many of those are the more tender varieties. Clematis are generally quite hardy, especially most of the large-flowered

Clematis are in the same family as buttercups and peonies

hybrids (hardy to Zone 4) and *C. viticella* (hardy to Zone 5). Many grow well in shade or on north walls and they thrive in most soils, although they prefer soil to be moisture-retentive and fertile.

BORDER TIME
The clouds of tiny white flowers of Clematis recta, a herbaceous species, add substance to a planting that includes the purple spikes of a salvia, an old-fashioned pink rose, and fennel.

THE CLEMATIS YEAR

A CAREFUL SELECTION of about a dozen species and hybrids will almost guarantee that you have at least one clematis in flower in the garden from early spring to autumn. Many types also have the advantage of feathery seedheads to follow the flowers, and some have fernlike or young purple foliage (*see chart, facing page*). To help you choose a mixture of clematis that will provide a succession of flowers, the gallery at the back of this book has been arranged in order of flowering season.

STARTING THE SEASON

For color at the start of the year, there are species that flower in late winter and early spring in mild areas or in a conservatory. Provide evergreen *Clematis cirrhosa* with some protection, and you will be rewarded by freckled, cream bells in late winter. By early spring, evergreen *C. armandii* and *C. indivisa* give a display of fragrant white

> Shining, fluffy seedheads
> in autumn extend the
> clematis season

flowers. Both may need the shelter of a wall. The alpinas and macropetalas also flower in early spring, producing seedheads to follow. Flowers vary from the simple bells of *C. alpina* to the intricate, nodding flowers of *C. macropetala*. By late spring,

▲ SWEET BEGINNINGS
Clematis armandii *carries clusters of flowers in early spring, which stand out well against the leathery evergreen leaves. A warm, sunny day will bring out their almond scent.*

◄ SPRING CHARM
Clematis alpina *'Rosy Pagoda' is an attractive and delicate-looking cultivar of this rather hardy early-flowering species.*

SUMMERTIME BLUES
'Lady Londesborough', an early large-flowered hybrid, is closely related to the species Clematis patens, used to breed many in this group.

AUTUMN HIGHLIGHTS
The seedheads of Clematis tibetana are among the most lustrous of any clematis, especially when caught by rays of autumn sunshine.

the vigorous *C. montana* is in flower, and some large-flowered hybrids, such as 'Lady Londesborough' (*above*), produce their first flush. Many flower again in late summer and early autumn, but their main flowering time is from late spring into early summer.

FROM SUMMER INTO AUTUMN

In summer, the large-flowered hybrids give a long display of blooms. Two groups dominate summer – the large-flowered Jackmanii types and small-flowered viticellas. *C. viticella* starts to bloom earlier than the

red-flowered *C. texensis*, while hybrids of the two offer an extended flowering season and a range of flower shapes and colors.

Many herbaceous and species clematis also flower in late summer. Two of the most popular climbing species are *C. tangutica* and *C. tibetana* subsp. *vernayi* (previously known as *C. orientalis*), which produce small, yellow bells, followed by seedheads. The herbaceous *C. heracleifolia* also flowers in late summer, while *C. terniflora* (sweet autumn clematis), formerly *C. paniculata*, perfumes the air in autumn.

CLEMATIS WITH EXTRA SEASONAL INTEREST

HANDSOME FOLIAGE

These all have leaves that are particularly attractive, even when the plant is not in flower:

C. aethusifolia Fernlike leaves
C. akebioides Fernlike leaves
C. cirrhosa var. *balearica* Finely cut evergreen foliage, turning bronze in winter
C. intricata Fernlike leaves
C. recta 'Purpurea' Purple foliage, turning green later in the season
C. tibetana Blue-green, finely cut foliage

DECORATIVE SEEDHEADS

The following all develop fluffy seedheads that enhance the plant long after flowering:

Alpinas (*see pages 50–51*)
Macropetalas (*see pages 50–51*)
C. 'Bill MacKenzie'
C. ladakhiana
C. tangutica
C. tibetana (*see photograph above*)
C. vitalba

THE COLOR RANGE

WITH ALMOST THE ENTIRE spectrum to choose from, clematis offer the gardener a vast selection of colors, from pale, subtle or dark shades to vivid, intense ones. Flowers vary from the small, primrose-scented, creamy green bells of *Clematis rehderiana* to the velvety, deep crimson blooms of the large-flowered hybrid 'Niobe' (*below*).

CLEMATIS TANGUTICA

COLOR THROUGH THE SEASONS

There is a white-flowered clematis for nearly every time of the year, from *Clematis armandii* in early spring; *C. alpina* 'White Moth', *C. montana* f. *grandiflora*, 'Miss Bateman', 'Alba Luxurians', and 'Huldine' through spring and summer; and *C. terniflora* in autumn. 'Marie Boisselot' has white flowers with cream stamens, while 'Miss Bateman' and 'James Mason' have purple stamens. Many of the wild species, such as the fragrant *C. flammula* and *C. potaninii*, have small white flowers. The colored foliage of the herbaceous *C. recta* 'Purpurea' is an ideal foil for its tiny white flowers in summer, while the white alpinas have light green leaves.

The flower colors of pale pink, pale mauve, and silvery blue hybrids, such as 'Silver Moon', 'Dawn', 'Miss Crawshay',

THE CLEMATIS PALETTE
As a genus, clematis provide the gardener with an extraordinary range of colors to choose from. Flowers vary from the purest white to the deepest, richest purple and often have prominent, colorful stamens that complement or contrast with the petals. A few clematis have dark foliage that sets off the flowers to even greater advantage.

CLEMATIS REHDERIANA

'MARIE BOISSELOT'

'NIOBE'

'ROYALTY'

'THE VAGABOND'

and 'Wada's Primrose', are likely to fade in bright sunlight, so it is best to plant them in light shade or next to a north wall. Pale early-flowering species, such as C. *montana* and C. *alpina*, flower when the sun is not so strong and are therefore less prone to fading. The purple-pink flowers of

Red flowers are at their best in full sun; pale colors need shade

C. *montana* 'Tetrarose' and 'Warwickshire Rose' have the advantage of bronze young foliage to set them off.

The dark hybrids, particularly the purples of the Jackmanii group and the near-true blues, such as 'Mrs. Cholmondeley' and 'Perle d'Azur', tend to flower most profusely in full sun, although 'Fireworks' and 'Lady Northcliffe' retain their flower color best when there is a little overhead shade.

The red-flowered hybrids, including 'Ville de Lyon', 'Rouge Cardinal', 'Niobe', and 'Ernest Markham', and the viticella types, such as 'Kermesina' and 'Madame Julia Correvon', flower most profusely and gain their best color intensity in full sun.

While there are cream large-flowered hybrids, the only true yellow clematis are in the tibetana group, producing small bells from mid- to late summer. The best choices are C. *tibetana*, C. *tangutica*, and 'Bill MacKenzie', which have fluffy seedheads after flowering. They are usually vigorous and suitable for growing up small trees or through shrubs. Softer yellow C. *serratifolia* is another late-flowering clematis.

CLEMATIS ALPINA 'WILLY'

'JOHN WARREN'

'COMTESSE DE BOUCHAUD'

'JACKMANII'

'W. E. GLADSTONE'

CLEMATIS ALPINA 'FRANCES RIVIS'

PLANNING COLOR COMBINATIONS

ONE OF THE MOST ATTRACTIVE WAYS to grow clematis in the garden is through other plants, mimicking how they twine through shrubs and trees in the wild. This technique provides infinite opportunities to play off their different habits, foliage, flower shapes, and colors against those of other plants. Combining the flowers of clematis with the foliage of shrubs that have already bloomed is an effective way to extend both plants' season of interest.

CREATING CONTRASTS

You can usually find room for a clematis even in a fully planted small garden – the rewards will be substantial in relation to the amount of planting space used. Use the opportunity to introduce flower colors that enhance the garden's vertical dimension.

Early-flowering clematis, such as alpinas and macropetalas, have abundant foliage that should be thinned to prevent it from smothering a host plant. Combining two clematis of the same species that have contrasting flower colors, such as C. *macropetala* 'Markham's Pink' with 'Blue Lagoon' or 'White Swan', is effective.

The early large-flowered hybrids bloom at the same time as late lilacs and roses (*see overleaf*). 'Guernsey Cream' has pale cream

MIXING COOL COLORS
The flowers of Clematis montana *and* Wisteria sinensis *create a harmonious blue and white display that is ideal for covering a strong pergola.*

Golden foliage highlights purple flowers, and silver harmonizes with blue

---

flowers that would complement a pink-flowered lilac. Purple- and silver-leaved foliage shrubs are perfect foils for clematis, showing off not only the color of the petals but their often prominent stamens.

Flowers in dusky and deep purple shades, such as those of C. *viticella* 'Mary Rose' or 'Royalty', are lost among dark green leaves. They will show up far better against golden foliage, such as that of *Sambucus nigra* 'Sutherland Gold' or *Philadelphus coronarius* 'Aureus'.

▲ LIGHT AGAINST DARK
The purple-leaved Cotinus
coggygria *is an ideal foil
for the white-flowered*
C. potaninii.

◄ GOLDEN LEAVES
The foliage of Choisya ternata
*'Sundance' enlivens the purple
flowers of* Clematis viticella.

CLEMATIS IN THE BORDER

Most of the midseason and late-flowering clematis can be grown through herbaceous plants in the border without overwhelming them. Hybrids such as 'The President', 'Madame Julia Correvon', and 'Duchess of Albany' (texensis group) can be pegged down and trained through plantings of phlox, artemisia, catmint, asters, fuchsias, or even grasses. There are many possible color combinations, from the subtle to the startling – such as red- and white-striped 'Dr. Ruppel' with the variegated phlox 'Norah Leigh'. You could also allow climbing clematis to trail through herbaceous species such as *C. integrifolia*.

RECOMMENDED COMBINATIONS

CLEMATIS AND PARTNER	EFFECT
'Asao' with the large shrub *Cotinus coggygria* 'Royal Purple'.	Abundant, large, deep pink flowers in early summer blend with the shrub's purple foliage.
'Ernest Markham' with *Berberis thunbergii* f. *atropurpurea*.	Red clematis flowers glow among the small purple leaves of the barberry from midsummer.
'Gipsy Queen' with *Helictotrichon sempervirens* (perennial grass).	From mid- to late summer, violet flowers thread between the blue-gray grass spikes.
'Etoile Violette' with *Pyrus salicifolia* 'Pendula', the weeping ornamental pear.	Masses of purple flowers stand out against silver foliage from late summer to autumn.
'Gravetye Beauty' with *Caryopteris* × *clandonensis* 'Heavenly Blue'.	In late summer, deep red flowers mingle with the soft blue blooms of the caryopteris.
Clematis × *durandii* with *Tropaeolum polyphyllum* (trailing perennial nasturtium).	Yellow flowers of the nasturtium contrast with the indigo-blue clematis blooms.

COMBINING CLEMATIS WITH ROSES

MOST SHRUB AND CLIMBING ROSES are remarkably similar to many clematis in their cultivation requirements and flowering season. In addition, their size, shape, and sturdy branching structure make them ideal supports for clematis. There are plenty of rose types to choose as hosts, from ramblers that can reach 10–30ft/3–10m, often with clusters of small pale flowers, to the large-flowered modern hybrids with their extensive color range.

PLANNING PLANT PARTNERS

The regular feeding and, if necessary, watering that enhances the flowering of roses will benefit clematis as well. You can also plan partnerships to make sure that the pruning times of both plants will coincide. Aim to avoid combining those clematis and roses that are prone to powdery mildew, since this is likely to spread from one plant to the other. *Clematis crispa* and the texensis

types are particularly susceptible to mildew. The early-flowering alpinas and macropetalas all have very dense growth and are ideal for training up and masking the usually bare lower stems of tall rambling and climbing roses. These clematis are less suitable for growing with small shrub roses, unless their bushy growth is thinned regularly. Clematis that flower earlier in the year and do not usually need pruning will benefit from thinning in late winter or early spring to five or six shoots, which are then tied to the rose bush. This will avoid the dense tangle that can result if they are left unpruned.

STRONG CONTRASTS
'Buff Beauty' rose supports 'Jackmanii Rubra', which has semidouble, pink flowers. The hybrid musk shrub roses are ideal hosts.

▲ SUBTLE BLENDS
The rosy lilac blooms of 'Hagley Hybrid' appear to give a second flowering to its host, Rosa glauca.

◄ PASTEL COMPANIONS
The pale lavender-blue flowers of 'Mrs. Cholmondeley' nestle among the glossy foliage of the climbing rose 'New Dawn', which has soft, shell-pink blooms.

As with roses, the flowers will be fewer but often larger, better spaced, and well formed.

All the large-flowered hybrids and the smaller-flowered viticellas that bloom in summer and early autumn are suitable for growing through roses. The early large-flowered hybrids bloom at the same time as most roses, from early to midsummer, so that planning color combinations can be

Late large-flowered hybrids and viticellas are ideal with old roses

very rewarding. Think about the effect you want to achieve: you may prefer a cool blend of pale or subtle shades or perhaps a contrasting display of vivid blooms.

The old-fashioned and species roses have few or no flowers by late summer and are ideal hosts for some clematis, including the late large-flowered hybrids and Jackmaniis and particularly the smaller-flowered

viticella hybrids. These have the advantage of being pruned hard every spring so that the roses can flower in early summer unencumbered. It is best to thin out their shoots as they regrow and space them evenly around the rose, or they tend to form bundles of shoots that sit lopsidedly on the rose, become overcrowded, and partially conceal the rose flowers.

GOOD COMBINATIONS

'Margot Koster', which has deep rosy-pink flowers, with the violet-lilac blooms of the rambling rose 'Veilchenblau'.

The silver-gray flowers of **'Silver Moon'** with the purple-pink rose 'Gertrude Jekyll'.

'Corona', which has pink flowers tinged purple-red, with the hybrid perpetual rose 'Reine des Violettes'.

The white flowers of **'Gillian Blades'** (*see p.58*) with the pink species rose Rosa × richardii.

Violet-flowered **'Royalty'** with the egg-yolk yellow blooms of the rose 'Alister Stella Gray'.

The all-white combination of **'Marie Boisselot'** and the rose 'Climbing Iceberg'.

CLEMATIS IN THE BORDER

IN PROVIDING IMPACT IN A BORDER PLANTING, clematis can surpass many shrubs and perennials. Choose from the range of herbaceous types, the early-flowering hybrids that can be grown on tripods within the border, and the late-flowering hybrids that will trail through mixed plantings. Although clematis are often added to existing border plantings, it is better to plan for their inclusion and to plant them in their own space rather than tucking them in as an afterthought.

HERBACEOUS CLEMATIS

The easiest clematis to include as part of a border planting are the herbaceous types, with compact growth that is more or less self-supporting compared with the climbers. These include quite bushy plants, such as *Clematis heracleifolia* and its cultivars. Thriving in sun or partial shade, they will reward you with bluish, fragrant flowers that sit above bunches of large, grapelike leaves. Other herbaceous varieties, such as *C. recta* 'Purpurea' and *C. integrifolia,*

require support from twigs, stakes, plant rings, or sturdy neighboring plants. They are suitable for growing by retaining walls or banks that can be partially concealed by attractive swaths of draping stems.

There are also clematis that make a good groundcover. *Clematis × jouiniana,* for example, can cover an area of up to 12ft/4m across and, when cut back in winter, leaves a large open space that is ideal for a spring bulb display. These can grow, bloom, and die back before the clematis spreads out again.

COOL BLUES
The violet-blue flowers of Clematis × durandii *add depth of color as they weave through a border planting of catmint* (Nepeta sibirica) *and goat's rue* (Galega). C. × durandii *is an attractive, semi-herbaceous clematis plant that requires support from twigs or neighboring plants.*

◄ ATTRACT WILDLIFE
*In late summer, this
combination of*
Clematis heracleifolia
var. davidiana *and*
Sedum *'Autumn Joy'
will attract butterflies
and bees.*

▼ PURE WHITES
*The small white
flowers of* Clematis
flammula *combine
effectively with those
of* Lychnis coronaria
*'Alba'. Both plants
thrive in drier parts
of the garden.*

CONSIDERING ALL THE OPTIONS

The early large-flowered hybrids are more tricky to grow among herbaceous plants, although they can be easily trained through shrubs. Alternatively, grow them over tripods placed within herbaceous plantings to give borders a spectacular vertical accent.

The viticellas, texensis, and the Jackmaniis can be grown on supports or allowed to scramble freely to add interest to virtually any late-flowering planting. Easy to grow, they need hard pruning in late winter or

> Training a large-flowered hybrid over a tripod adds height to a border

early spring, at the same time as most herbaceous perennials. Where they are to trail through other plants, it is important to thin and space out the new shoots as they grow, pegging them down into the soil (*see p.33*) or just threading them through neighboring plants; otherwise, clumps of shoots can smother host plants. Most strong-growing herbaceous plants, such as phlox or asters, however, can support the weight of a clematis shoot or two.

CHOOSING HOST TREES AND SHRUBS

TREES AND SHRUBS MAKE USEFUL PARTNERS for clematis, which use them as a frame to twine around as they grow upward to reach the light. In their flowering season, clematis provide color and interest, perhaps decorating a bare trunk or forming a canopy over branches or arching stems. There are few sights as beautiful in the garden as a large tree draped in the white or pale pink flowers of a *Clematis montana*. Some species, such as *C. terniflora*, can cover their host entirely.

ESTABLISHING HEALTHY PLANTS

When using a tree or a shrub as a host plant, make sure that its root system is not competing with the clematis for water and nutrients. To do this, plant the clematis away from the base of the host and mulch with well-rotted manure each spring. Consider the size of the host plant in relation to the vigor of the clematis. A shrub or small tree needs to be able to bear the weight of the clematis and not be smothered by it.

Avoid planting clematis near trees with dense root systems, such as beech and maple. Old conifers that have dry soil under their canopies can be used to provide support if the clematis is planted 3–6ft/1–2m outside the "drip line" (the edge of the canopy and the rain shadow it casts). The clematis can be trained over the ground, along a length of rope, or up a stake to reach the tree.

▲ COVERING A BARE TREE TRUNK
Clematis alpina *combines well with trees, although it requires help to reach the lower branches. Stakes or twine used for training the stems will soon be covered by growth.*

◄ AN EFFECTIVE FOLIAGE BACKDROP
Clematis can be used to enliven a shrub that has already flowered, such as in this planting of 'Cardinal Wyszynski' with a rhododendron.

A LONG SHOW
A lilac can act as the perfect host for clematis. In this planting, a combination of two hybrid clematis will bloom in summer, after the lilac has finished flowering. 'Fireworks' can grow up to 10ft/3m high into the shrub, while 'Lady Northcliffe' clambers around the lower branches.

PLANNING PERFECT PARTNERSHIPS

Almost all the large-flowered hybrids, viticellas, and compact species clematis make good partners for established shrubs that reach 6–15ft/2–5m. The alpinas and macropetalas are best for growing among small trees that have low, forking branches, such as maple or magnolia.

To scramble over large, mature trees, choose *C. montana* for spring and early summer flowers, and *C. potaninii* or 'Paul Farges' for small white flowers in late summer and autumn. Alternatively, *C. tangutica* and 'Bill MacKenzie', with yellow bells in late summer and autumn, can reach 15–24ft/5–7m in height. Many of the montanas grow to 24ft/8m or more, so be sure that the tree is large enough not be too overwhelmed by such a vigorous clematis. It is difficult to get access to prune tangled, overdense growth once it is scrambling high through the branches of a tall tree.

When planting a clematis with a shrub, consider the flowering time of each plant, how they will complement one another, and any pruning methods involved. Late summer- and autumn-flowering clematis need hard pruning, but the lower stems attached to the tree or shrub can often be left unpruned to give the new shoots a head start each year.

GOOD HOSTS FOR CLEMATIS

TREES	SHRUBS
Acer tataricum subsp. *ginnala*	Barberries, such as *Berberis thunbergii*
Arborvitaes, such as *Thuja occidentalis*	Buddleias, such as *B. alternifolia* 'Argentea'
Catalpa bignonioides 'Aurea'	Ceanothus, such as *C.* 'Cascade'
Chamaecyparis, such as *C. nootkatensis* 'Pendula'	Cotinus, such as *C. coggygria* 'Royal Purple'
Hollies, such as *Ilex opaca*	*Hydrangea aspera* Villosa Group
Magnolia × *soulangeana*	Junipers, such as *Juniperus* 'Pfitzeriana Aurea'
Crabapples, such as *Malus* × *zumi* 'Golden Hornet'	Lilacs, such as *Syringa vulgaris* 'Madame Lemoine'
Pines, such as *Pinus sylvestris*	Mock oranges, such as *Philadelphus* 'Belle Etoile'
Weeping pear (*Pyrus salicifolia* 'Pendula')	Rhododendrons, such as *R.* 'Sappho'
Sorbus, such as *S. aucuparia* and cultivars	Yews, such as *Taxus* × *media* 'Hicksii'

COVERING VERTICAL SURFACES

CLEMATIS GROWING ON WALLS, fences, trellises, and obelisks are a familiar and attractive sight. With the exception of roses, there are few plants that can match clematis in beauty and usefulness for clothing vertical surfaces. Most clematis are reasonably lightweight in their growth and climb easily, their leaf tendrils needing to gain only a little support from a few vine eyes threaded with garden twine or wire to reach the top of a wall.

SUPPORTING CLEMATIS

For dense cover, there are many types of meshlike materials available as supports, from very lightweight plastic netting to a wooden trellis. However, other climbing plants, particularly roses, make equally good supports. The foliage of some clematis, particularly the early-flowering hybrids, can begin to look rather ratty by the end of the summer. Growing them through other plants can disguise or even conceal this disappointing trait.

Some clematis have superb foliage, especially the evergreen *Clematis armandii*, which needs plenty of shelter to protect its glossy, leathery leaves. Likewise, *C. cirrhosa* (the winter-flowering clematis) and its variations have attractive, finely cut foliage and are best appreciated growing over an arch or arbor so that you can enjoy looking up into the freckled bells.

▲ OVER A PILLAR
Two of the most reliable and popular clematis, the striped 'Nelly Moser' and 'The President', conceal a brick pillar with the aid of strands of wire.

◄ SHELTERED SITE
Clematis armandii
'Apple Blossom' benefits from the protection of a wall to produce its clusters of white flowers offset by glossy foliage.

C. montana has purple-leaved forms, such as 'Warwickshire Rose', and can reach 30ft/10m. Its dense growth makes it useful for covering unsightly outbuildings.

For exposed walls and fences up to 6–10ft/2–3m high, the best choices are the alpinas and macropetalas. These are valuable for their fresh foliage, spring flowers, and fluffy seedheads in summer.

Early large-flowered hybrids, such as 'Marie Boisselot', often have very lanky growth and bloom only at the top. It is

> A montana makes fine camouflage for an ugly building or wall

often worth spiraling the shoots of these clematis around tripods or obelisks to encourage them to produce flowers more evenly over the plant. This technique does not work so well for late-flowering hybrids, which have much more vigorous growth. Their shoots tend to leap up vertically at so fast a rate as to defy training. Instead, combine them with other climbing plants, such as honeysuckle or roses, so that they can clamber freely.

▲ MAXIMUM COVERAGE
Clematis montana *is a vigorous species that is capable of weaving through and over fences and covering unsightly buildings. In late spring it bursts into flower.*

▼ OBELISK OF COLOR
'Etoile Violette' and the sweet pea 'Noel Sutton' (an annual) are both vigorous plants that grow quickly to cover a wooden obelisk, putting on a colorful summer show.

GROWING CLEMATIS IN CONTAINERS

CLEMATIS ARE EASY TO GROW IN CONTAINERS, allowing their beauty to be enjoyed on patios, balconies, and terraces. Only the most vigorous, such as the montanas, are really impractical for container-growing. Any style of pot or planter you choose can be combined with a climbing plant support, from the wide range of tripods, obelisks, and woven willow cones to intricate wire globes. (To make your own wire globe, *see pages 36–37.*)

CONSIDERING PRACTICALITIES

The more vigorous the clematis, the bigger the container you will need; even with some of the newer, very compact clematis, always make sure that containers are at least 18in/45cm deep and wide. It is best to fill them with a soil-based mix blended with some slow-release fertilizer. Regular watering will be essential, but covering the soil mix with a pebble or cocoa-shell mulch will help conserve moisture.

Planting a two-year-old clematis with a well-developed root system in a large pot will give you a good display in the first year. Every following year, scrape away the top 4in/10cm of soil mix, being careful not to damage the roots of the plant, and replace with fresh mix. To encourage the most flowers, feed the clematis throughout

▲ PYRAMID OF EXOTIC BLOOMS
The rather tender Clematis florida *'Sieboldii' grows well in containers, its eye-catching flowers shown to great effect.*

◀ AN EXUBERANT DISPLAY
To get value from a container display, choose a reliable clematis with a long flowering period, such as 'Comtesse de Bouchaud'.

the growing season with a liquid seaweed fertilizer or a tomato fertilizer.

Choose clematis that will give maximum value in terms of display. 'Arabella', for example, has a very long flowering season and grows to only 3–6ft/1–2m. 'Niobe' is also a good choice because it can be

During the summer, containers may need watering every day

encouraged with light pruning to give a prolonged flowering. Combining one early- and one late-flowering clematis gives a long display, but you must take extra care when pruning. Alternatively, planting two clematis with the same flowering season allows you to create attractive color combinations.

GOOD CHOICES

Alpinas (*see pp.50–51*)
Macropetalas (*see pp.50–51*)
Viticellas (*see pp.66–67*)
Clematis florida **'Flore Pleno'** Double white
'Barbara Dibley' Purple-red, deeper midribs
'Beauty of Worcester' Intense blue
'Bees' Jubilee' (*see p.57*) Pink with deeper bars
'Carnaby' (*see p.57*) Deep pink
'Comtesse de Bouchaud' (*see p.62*) Pink
'Countess of Lovelace' (*see p.61*) Lilac-blue
'Elsa Späth' (*see p.54*) Deep blue
'H. F. Young' (*see p.54*) Mid-blue
'Hagley Hybrid' (*see p.62*) Pale mauve-pink
'John Huxtable' Violet-blue flowers
'Miss Bateman' (*see p.58*) White
'Mrs. George Jackman' (*see p.61*) White
'Niobe' (*see p.59*) Ruby red
'Perle d'Azur' (*see p.8*) Clear blue flowers
'Proteus' (*see p.61*) Mauve-pink, variable

▲ ALPINE CLEMATIS
A tender, evergreen clematis from New Zealand, C. × cartmanii 'Joe' needs to be kept dry and protected in winter. Grown in a pot, it can be moved easily.

◀ A FOCAL POINT
Clematis macropetala *'Maidwell Hall' cascades from an urn. Its stems are trained over netting that has been draped over the sides of the urn.*

CARING FOR YOUR CLEMATIS

PRIOR TO PLANTING

WITH SO MANY LOVELY CLEMATIS becoming available at many garden centers, it can be hard to resist buying on impulse. But it's important to be sure what type of clematis it is, so that you know when it's going to flower and to which pruning group it belongs. Try always to have a site in mind, to know how your clematis will be supported, and to have supports ready in place.

SELECTING THE BEST PLANTS

Two-year-old clematis, like the one on the right, are by far the easiest to establish in the garden and, for the speed at which they will grow, are well worth paying a little more for. Look for plants that have more than one stem growing from the base, and healthy foliage. Roots should be sufficiently developed for you to see them through the holes in the base of the pot, but not growing out of the holes and into the display bed. Clematis are unwieldy to transport: take care of the plant's fragile stems, and do not remove any protective stake caps until you have finished planting.

A PROMISING PLANT
Look carefully before you decide whether to buy – height is not as important as the number and vigor of the plant's shoots. It need not have flower buds, though two-year-old plants may have plenty.

Foliage should cover the whole plant

Look for a number of growing shoots

The roots should be strong and healthy

BUYING TIPS

• Although container-grown clematis can be planted all season, don't buy and plant them during hot spells when the soil is dry.

• The popularity of clematis means that suppliers may restock frequently, so don't accept a bad plant; wait for new ones to be delivered, or ask if you can place an order.

• If you can't find a particular clematis, consider mail-order specialists; ask them what age the plant they send will be.

◀ GRAND FINALE *Enchanting autumn seedheads follow* Clematis tibetana's *yellow bells.*

PUTTING UP A TRELLIS

MOST CLEMATIS NEED THIN SUPPORTS such as wires or slats to twine around. Trellising is a simple and lasting solution for wall-training. The method below enables you to lower the trellis with the clematis clinging onto it, should you need to reach the wall for maintenance. Use the brick courses as a guide to ensure that the trellis is (or at least looks!) straight. There are ready-to-assemble packs of trellis strips to hide downspouts, if you wish.

ATTACHING A TRELLIS TO A WALL

YOU NEED:

MATERIALS
- Trellis panel
- 2 1½×1in/3.5×2.5cm slats, the width of the panel in length
- 6 2in/50mm screws
- Wall anchors
- 2 hinges, plus screws
- 2 hooks and eyes

TOOLS
- Pencil
- Metal tape measure
- Drill (preferably electric) with wood and masonry bits
- Hammer
- Awl
- Screwdriver

1 **Hold** the trellis panel in position against the wall. Align the edges with the straight lines of the brickwork. Mark the position of the trellis panel at the top and lower edges, and on each side.

2 **Drill** 3 holes in each slat, one at each end and one in the center, ready for screwing to the wall. Drill onto a scrap of wood, placed beneath the slat.

3 **Hold** the slats against the wall, aligning the edges with the positional marks for the trellis.

4 **Mark the position** of the screwholes on the wall, before removing the slats. Drill holes in the wall (*see inset*), then hammer in the wall anchors.

5 **Screw the top** slat securely to the wall, first checking again that its upper edge aligns with the positional marks for the trellis.

6 Screw the hinges onto the lower edge of the bottom slat, having started the holes using an awl. Position the slat to align with the positional marks for the trellis, then screw securely to the wall.

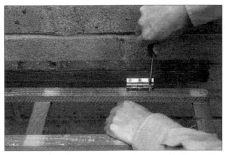

7 Hold the base of the trellis panel alongside the lower slat, aligning the ends. Screw the hinges attached to the slat to the bottom of the trellis panel (*see above*). You may need to support the trellis panel to do this.

8 Raise the trellis into position to check that it aligns with the top slat. Then screw hooks into each end of the top slat and eyes into each end of the trellis panel (*see inset*) to hold it in place.

ATTACHING A TRELLIS KIT TO A DOWNSPOUT

1 Lay out the 3 strips of trellis from the pack, interlocking the edges of the lattice. Fasten them together temporarily with rubber bands.

2 Position the trellis around the downspout and fasten in place with the clips provided in the pack. Remove the rubber bands.

3 Tie the clematis shoots onto the trellis with soft twine. Use figure-eight knots to allow the stem to expand and move slightly.

PLANTING AND WATERING

THE BEST TIMES TO PLANT CLEMATIS are autumn or early spring, although much of the year is possible as long as you water frequently in the first summer. Incorporate a watering system (*see opposite*) at the planting stage. Although most clematis need light and some sun to flower well, their roots like to be kept cool. A mulch helps shade the roots and conserve moisture. Clematis prefer well-drained soil and need plentiful feeding and watering until established.

PLANTING CLEMATIS BY A WALL OR FENCE

When planting a clematis against a wall, position it well away from the base (up to 12in/30cm), especially where there is overhang from gutters or other structures. The soil under a wall is generally very dry. Dig a deep hole so that, once planted, the lowest 4–8in/10–20cm of the clematis stems are below the soil surface. Deep planting encourages new shoots to develop at the base should you need to cut the clematis back. If the soil is heavy, improve the drainage by working some fine grit or sharp sand into the soil at the base of the planting hole. Mix in plenty of well-rotted manure or compost and some bonemeal (wear gloves when handling) with the soil, especially at the bottom of the hole. Water well and mulch the surface. It is best not to use bark chips as a mulch because they can harbor pests such as slugs and earwigs.

SHADING PLANT ROOTS
• A mulch of well-rotted manure or leaf-mold looks best in a border or with shrubs.
• A pebble or gravel mulch is ideal by a wall.
• Low-growing plants growing in front of the clematis will shield the roots from the sun.

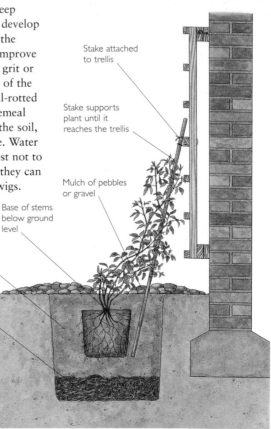

Stake attached to trellis

Stake supports plant until it reaches the trellis

Mulch of pebbles or gravel

Base of stems below ground level

Well-rotted manure and bonemeal mixed with the soil

Well-rotted manure improves soil structure and encourages deep rooting

PLANTING DEEPLY
Plant clematis deeply, enriching the soil with well-rotted manure or compost. Mulching around the base of the plant shades the roots and conserves moisture.

PLANTING A CLEMATIS TO GROW INTO A SHRUB

Plant the clematis away from its host so that there is less competition for food and moisture. The clematis needs to be outside the rainshadow and drip line created by the shrub. If the shrub is not fully grown, you must take its eventual spread into account; a vigorous clematis can easily travel up to 6ft/2m, if necessary, before reaching its host.

1 **Dig a generous hole** at least 18in/45cm wide and deep. Mix well-rotted manure or compost into the soil.

2 **Mark** the ground level with a horizontal stake. Put in the clematis; check that at least 4in/10cm of stem is buried.

3 **Mulch** the area with well-rotted manure or compost after watering in. Lean the stake toward the shrub.

WATERING CLEMATIS

Most clematis need plenty of moisture in order to thrive. This is particularly important while the plant is getting established. To make watering as efficient as possible, it is a good idea to bury a piece of pipe or a flower pot alongside the clematis at planting time; pouring the water into it will ensure that it reaches the plant's roots. Simply watering around the base of the plant can encourage roots to form near the soil surface, making the plant more likely to suffer from drought. Once a mulch has been laid it is, in any case, harder for water to penetrate the ground, and in hot weather a lot can be lost through evaporation.

Once established, a clematis should flourish without watering if the soil has been enriched with organic matter (such as rotted manure), which encourages good, deep root growth. Renew mulches as necessary.

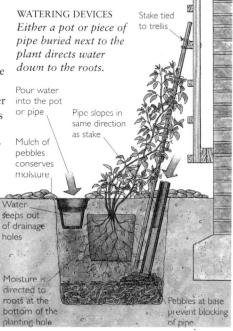

WATERING DEVICES
Either a pot or piece of pipe buried next to the plant directs water down to the roots.

Stake tied to trellis

Pour water into the pot or pipe

Pipe slopes in same direction as stake

Mulch of pebbles conserves moisture

Water seeps out of drainage holes

Moisture is directed to roots at the bottom of the planting hole

Pebbles at base prevent blocking of pipe

TRAINING CLEMATIS

EXCEPT FOR THE HERBACEOUS TYPES, clematis naturally twine readily around the stems of a host plant or other support. This may make training seem unnecessary. However, most flower better and more profusely if trained in some way, with their stems spread evenly over a trellis or shrub, or pegged along the ground. If left to themselves, plants tend to become tangled, resulting in smaller and fewer flowers that are partly obscured by crowded foliage.

TYING IN CLEMATIS STEMS

Initially, it is best to tie the stems of a newly planted clematis to its support, then it will start to attach itself using its twining leaf stalks. Use garden twine or twist ties, but take care, since the stems are very fragile. Plants flower more evenly if the main stems can be trained horizontally at first, or spiraled around a pillar or obelisk. Late-flowering hybrids grow too quickly to make it worth trying to train in this way.

IDEAS FOR SUPPORTS

• Vertical wires stretched between eyes screwed into a wall or the pillars of a pergola, or wide-gauge wire netting (ask for turkey wire), are less obtrusive than a trellis.

• Metal obelisks, often supplied complete with wire panels for better coverage.

• Twig and branch tepees, bought already made or constructed from pliable stems.

▲ THE TWINING HABIT OF CLEMATIS
Clematis cling by twining their leaf stalks around wires, strings, or stems of host plants. You just need to encourage the natural process.

► USING FIGURE-EIGHT KNOTS
When tying with string, take care with the brittle stems and use loose figure-eight knots to prevent chafing against the support.

PEGGING DOWN A CLEMATIS IN THE BORDER

Late-flowering clematis, especially the texensis and viticella hybrids, can look good grown along the ground in borders or beds. Here they spread out, twining through the stems of shrubs and herbaceous plants or forming an attractive, light groundcover. It is important to direct these clematis, pegging them down where you want them to flower. If left untrained, their stems tend to form a tight tangle and create a far less elegant display, with flowers partially lost among the foliage. The technique involved is very straightforward. All you need to pin the stems along the ground are some 6–7in/ 15–18cm lengths of wire bent into hooks (*right*).

WIRE HOOKS

WHEN TO START PEGGING DOWN
The new growth of Clematis viticella *tends to leap up in a confused tangle in spring. When the growth is about 1½–3ft/50cm–1m long, it is time to start training it.*

1 **Pull the stems** apart gently, selecting about a third of them to peg down. Do not worry if some shoots break in the process. Cut the remainder close to the ground.

2 **Using the wire hooks,** peg down the stems around the plant, inserting a hook every 1½ft/50cm or so. You can encourage the growth in any direction you wish.

3 **Train the stems** once again as they grow, then leave the clematis to its own devices. By mid- to late summer a well-established, vigorous plant like this will cover an area of about 12–1.5ft/4–5m in blooms. New shoots will also emerge from the center of the plant to flower later in the season.

LOOKING AFTER CLEMATIS

IF CLEMATIS ARE GIVEN A GOOD START by thorough preparation at the planting stage, they will not demand a great deal of time and attention in later years. Feed and water plants generously in their first season, but, once established, they will need little more than a good mulch of rotted manure each spring. Even pruning (*see pp.38–43*) is not essential for every type of clematis.

AT A GLANCE	WHAT TO DO
SPRING • Prune • Feed plants • Renew mulches	Prune (*see pp.38–43*) to encourage healthy growth and more flowers. Mulch with well-rotted cow or horse manure to feed plants and conserve moisture. Where pebble or gravel mulches have been laid, use pelleted chicken manure or liquid seaweed fertilizer. Renew stone mulches if necessary to conserve moisture, shade roots, and keep down weeds.
SUMMER • Feed plants in containers • Train new shoots • Water young plants • Take cuttings	Feed clematis in pots with liquid seaweed or tomato fertilizer. This will also help clematis in the garden that are not thriving. Train new shoots to prevent them from becoming tangled and to spread growth evenly over a host òr support. Water young plants until they are established. Before midsummer, take cuttings (*see pp.44–45*) of clematis you wish to propagate.
AUTUMN • Collect seed • Hard-prune Group 3 clematis if required	Gather seedheads (*see pp.46–47*) for sowing. If the brown stems of a Group 3 clematis mar the attractiveness of a host shrub in winter, the stems can be safely cut back hard (*see p.43*) once they have died down; otherwise, wait until spring.
WINTER • Protect marginally hardy clematis against cold	Cover clematis with straw or thick, small-mesh netting. Move plants in containers into a greenhouse or conservatory.

GUARDING AGAINST PESTS

Good general care of plants helps to promote their health and makes them less likely to succumb to pests. There are also preventive measures that will deter the pests most often associated with clematis –

EARWIG DAMAGE
Earwigs take notches out of the sides of flowers and leaves. Good garden hygiene will discourage them from living under old vegetation.

slugs, mice, earwigs, and aphids. Slugs are the most common pests – they damage new shoots, sometimes surprisingly high up on plants. Discourage them by placing sharp grit around the base of the plant or use beer traps. Also remove garden debris and old hollow stems that can harbor both slugs and earwigs.

Mice can chew plants as they grow. The plants usually recover, but not until a whole season later. Covering young shoots with chicken wire will act as a deterrent. You can pinch off shoots badly infested by aphids, or spray with insecticidal soap.

Keeping Clematis Healthy

Healthy, vigorous plants are much more resistant to disease. Bear in mind, too, that correct pruning not only helps promote better flowering but also includes cutting out dead and damaged wood, thus improving air circulation and removing potential entry points for infection.

Many clematis, especially the early- and late-flowering species and the viticella hybrids, are virtually trouble-free. However, overbreeding of the large-flowered hybrids has meant that some have become liable to clematis wilt and others to mildew.

Clematis wilt looks disastrous, but the plant may be saved. Cut out all affected stems, if necessary right down to the ground, and feed the plant with liquid seaweed fertilizer. If the clematis is planted deeply (*see p.30*), it may reshoot from below ground.

Mildew is best discouraged by good air circulation. Do not train clematis prone to mildew flat against walls or among roses. Slime flux is a rare disease that usually affects only *Clematis montana*. Prune and destroy the affected wood. If the plant dies, do not replant a clematis in the same spot.

CLEMATIS WILT
The first sign of this disease is the wilting of some shoots or even the entire plant. It most often occurs in early summer, when the plant is full of young growth and flower buds. The diseased shoots turn brown and collapse.

SLIME FLUX
This disease is rare but can be fatal; it causes a slimy, saplike substance to ooze thickly from the stems near the base of the plant.

MILDEW ON CLEMATIS
Texensis hybrids and closely related species, such as Clematis addisonii *and C. reticulata, are prone to this grayish fungal infection.*

A CLEMATIS GLOBE

T HE TWINING HABIT of clematis can be utilized to create architectural shapes over supporting wire structures. A wire globe clothed in a clematis makes a simple but very striking feature. The technique is easy, with new shoots being trained in as the clematis grows to obscure the wire. In the flowering season, you will be rewarded by a sphere of blooms and, with some clematis, a second flush later in the year.

MAKING A WIRE GLOBE

1 **Insert 3 stakes** firmly into the soil mix, spacing them evenly around the clematis. Tie them at the top with wire to form a tepee.

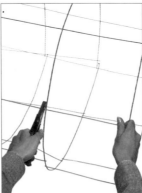

Position stakes near the edge of the container

2 **Cut the mesh** to form 6 ladderlike strips 60in/ 1.4m long. Cut with 2 prongs at both ends for inserting into the soil mix and to the stakes.

YOU NEED:

MATERIALS
• 15–18in/38–46cm pot with drainage hole
• Clematis. Choose a compact type, (*see pp.24–25*) and plant it attached to the support it came with
• 3 bamboo stakes, approximately 36in/1m long
• Wide-gauge (8in/20cm mesh) galvanized wire netting, 88×60in/220×140cm

TOOLS
• Pliers or nippers for cutting wire

3 **Bend the prongs** at the bottom of the first wire strip inward, and insert them securely into the soil mix at the edge of the container. Form the strip into a semicircular shape.

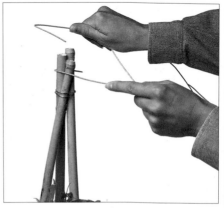

4 **Shape the wire ends** at the top of the strip into hooks that will fit around the tops of the stakes. Twist the ends together to hold the wire securely on the stakes.

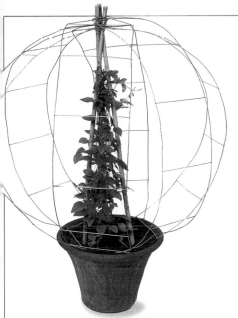

5 **Complete the wire globe** by doing the remaining 5 wire strips in the same way, spacing them evenly around the edges of the container to form a balloon shape.

6 **Detach and thread the stems** through to the outside along the base of the globe. Start weaving them in and out of the wires. Continue to direct the stems as they grow.

A SPHERE OF FLOWERS
Clematis florida *'Flore Pleno'* conceals the frame beneath abundant double white flowers. Initially, take the stems in a horizontal or diagonal direction to encourage the clematis to produce flowers on the bottom half of the globe as well as the top.

PRACTICAL TIPS

• Clematis that are more tender, such as *C. florida* 'Flore Pleno', may need to be moved into a greenhouse or conservatory for protection in winter.

• In spring, scrape away the top of the soil mix and apply a fresh layer. Add some slow-release fertilizer.

• Prune the clematis according to its group, and train new stems around the globe as they grow.

PRUNING CLEMATIS

CLEMATIS VARY IN THEIR FLOWERING TIMES and differ in their pruning requirements. They are generally divided into three main pruning groups. Clematis that flower in spring require little pruning (Pruning Group 1), those that flower in early summer require light pruning (Pruning Group 2), and those that flower from midsummer onward require hard pruning (Pruning Group 3). The following pages list clematis in each group and show how to prune them.

FLOWERING TIME AND PRUNING

The way in which the different clematis are pruned relates to the age of wood on which they bear their flowers.

PRUNING GROUP 1 clematis flower in spring on stems that grew and ripened in the previous year, so any pruning removes potential flowering wood. Therefore, they are pruned only to thin them when really necessary – which makes them great for covering eyesores year-round or training into less accessible places where regular access would be inconvenient.

PRUNING GROUP 2 includes all the large-flowered hybrids that bloom in early summer. Their flowers are borne on sideshoots that grow from the previous year's ripened stems. As with Group 1, therefore, they must not be hard-pruned if flowers are to form – but light pruning will stimulate more flowering sideshoots on the stems that remain. They should be sited and trained so that you can gain access to the stems to prune lightly in late winter.

PRUNING GROUP 3, the midseason to late-flowering clematis, are the easiest for gardeners who hate making pruning decisions – you simply cut everything back in late winter or early spring. Strong new stems will then grow vigorously and bear flowers all in a single season.

WHEN TO PRUNE CLEMATIS

PRUNING GROUP 1	PRUNING GROUP 2	PRUNING GROUP 3
Prune only to thin, if necessary, in late winter or after flowering (*see p.40*). The following can also be hard-pruned after flowering: Alpinas Macropetalas *Clematis barbellata* *Clematis cirrhosa* *Clematis koreana* *Clematis* 'Pruinina' Never cut these hard back into old, dark wood: Montanas *Clematis armandii* *Clematis chrysocoma* *Clematis gracilifolia* *Clematis × vedrariensis*	Prune lightly in late winter to strong growth and buds, leaving a good framework (*see p.41*). This group includes all the early large-flowered hybrids.	Prune hard in late winter/ early spring, cutting all stems back (*see p.43*). This group includes all the late large-flowered hybrids, the mid- to late-flowering species, and herbaceous clematis.

'MISS BATEMAN'

'BILL MACKENZIE'

How to Prune Clematis

Always use sharp pruners when pruning, and position cuts just above a leaf joint (node), taking care not to damage any new buds or shoots sprouting from it if growth has already begun. If you have a choice of where to prune to, as on the early large-flowered hybrids, choose a really strong-looking bud or shoot. When pruning out old, unproductive growth, make the cut close to a branching point. Alternatively, prune to the ground to encourage new growth from below the soil surface.

PRUNING OUT OLD GROWTH
Prune down to a branching point, leaving a strong framework. Make a clean cut without leaving snags.

LIGHT PRUNING
In late winter, prune directly above a pair of strong buds. The new spring shoots indicate the best place to prune.

HARD PRUNING
Cut immediately above the lowest pair of strong buds on each stem – this will be 6–12in/ 15–30cm above soil level.

Renovating Clematis

If you take over an old garden, there may be massive tangles of overgrown clematis to deal with. Almost all clematis except the montanas and early large-flowered hybrids can be cut back to the ground, so if you don't know what you have inherited, the safest course is to renovate it as if it were one of these. Take the entire plant off its host plant or trellis, if necessary, then remove almost all the old growth and all the dense twigs and old seedheads. Retain 3–5 6ft/2m-long shoots to train back in place.

A NEGLECTED CLEMATIS

AFTER RENOVATION

AN OVERGROWN CLEMATIS
On the far left, an old large-flowered hybrid, unpruned for over three years, is a typical problem that you may need to tackle. It can be hard to know where to start, but be brave. Remove almost all the old growth, retaining only a few good long shoots. These may need fanning out slightly and retraining – here, they have been guided back into the branches of a conifer. The clematis should flower in the summer, helping you identify it if necessary.

PRUNING GROUP 1

It is not essential to prune clematis in this group, but they do benefit from occasional thinning (*see below*) to reinvigorate them and to reduce their weight and bulk – particularly where they are grown to form swaths over arbors, gates, and arches. Most can also be cut back hard if necessary, except for *Clematis montana*, which dislikes hard pruning into old wood. To renovate montanas, you can cut away all the old, dense, twiggy growth, but always leave some strong stems intact.

1 **Flowering** on the previous year's wood, Group 1 clematis must not be pruned too hard. Thin dense growth, cutting stems back to a pair of buds or to the point of origin.

2 **Cut back** any weak or damaged growth to strong buds or to its base.

CLEMATIS IN PRUNING GROUP 1

Clematis alpina	*Clematis armandii*	*Clematis macropetala*	'Mayleen'
'Columbine'	'Apple Blossom'	'Blue Bird'	'Picton's Variety'
'Constance'	'Snowdrift'	'Jan Lindmark'	var. *rubens*
'Frances Rivis'	*Clematis* × *cartmanii*	'Lagoon' (syn. 'Blue	var. *sericea*
'Frankie'	'Joe'	Lagoon')	'Tetrarose'
'Helsingborg'	*Clematis chrysocoma*	'Maidwell Hall'	'Warwickshire Rose'
'Pink Flamingo'	*Clematis cirrhosa*	'Markham's Pink'	var. *wilsonii*
'Rosy Pagoda'	var. *balearica*	*Clematis montana*	'Pruinina'
'Ruby'	'Freckles'	'Broughton Star'	'Rosie O'Grady'
subsp. *sibirica*	'Wisley Cream'	'Elizabeth'	'White Swan'
'White Moth'	*Clematis gracilifolia*	'Fragrant Spring'	
'Tage Lundell'	*Clematis indivisa*	'Freda'	
'Willy'	*Clematis koreana*	f. *grandiflora*	
	f. *lutea*	'Marjorie'	

PRUNING GROUP 2

This group is composed entirely of the early large-flowered hybrids (*see next page*), including those with double flowers, whose second flush later in the summer produces only single blooms. Although Group 2 clematis can be left unpruned, the flowers are larger and foliage is healthier on well-pruned plants.

The clematis in this group require light pruning in late winter or early spring to thin the plant down to a framework of well-spaced one- or two-year-old stems. Prune out any weak growth and all the twiggy sideshoots. This will help stimulate new shoots and encourage more prolific flowering. The fat leaf-axil buds that appear in early spring produce the first batch of flowers. You can prolong the flowering season of these clematis if you stagger the pruning by cutting back some shoots to healthy buds later than others (*see p.43*). There will not be as many flowers in the main flush as with the standard pruning procedure, but the flowering period will be longer overall.

Avoid using shrubs such as buddleia, caryopteris, or perovskia, which are cut back hard in spring, to support a Group 2 clematis. It will be nearly impossible to prune the shrub once the clematis has started twining through it.

Alternatively, Group 2 clematis can be grown with minimal pruning, cutting back hard every three or four years. The first flush of flowers is lost after hard pruning, but the second has larger, more plentiful blooms.

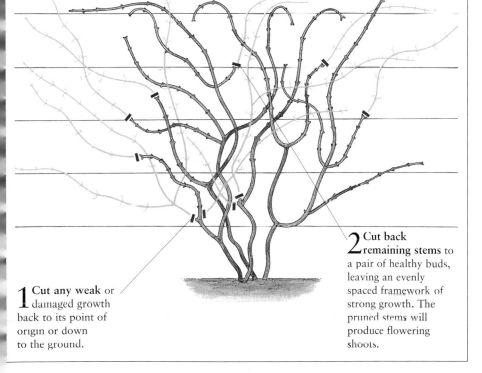

1 Cut any weak or damaged growth back to its point of origin or down to the ground.

2 Cut back remaining stems to a pair of healthy buds, leaving an evenly spaced framework of strong growth. The pruned stems will produce flowering shoots.

CLEMATIS IN PRUNING GROUP 2

Clematis patens
'Andromeda'
'Arctic Queen'
'Asao'
'Barbara Dibley'
'Barbara Jackman'
'Beauty of Richmond'
'Beauty of Worcester'
'Bees' Jubilee'
'Belle Nantaise'
'Belle of Woking'
'Blue Ravine'
'Bracebridge Star'
'Burma Star'
'Chalcedony'
'Cardinal Wyszynski'
'Carnaby'
'Carnival Queen'
'Charissima'
'Corona'
'Countess of Lovelace'
'Crimson King'
'Daniel Deronda'
'Dawn'
'Doctor Ruppel'
'Duchess of Edinburgh'
'Duchess of Sutherland'
'Edith'
'Edouard Desfossé'

'Elsa Späth'
'Empress of India'
'Etoile de Malicorne'
'Etoile de Paris'
'Fair Rosamond'
'Fairy Queen'
'Fireworks'
'Fuji-musume'
'Général Sikorski'
'Gillian Blades'
'Glynderek'
'Guernsey Cream'
'Haku-ôkan'
'H.F. Young'
'Henryi'
'Horn of Plenty'
'Jackmanii Alba'
'Jackmanii Rubra'
'James Mason'
'Joan Picton'
'John Paul II' (syn.
     'Jan Pawel II')
'John Warren'
'Kathleen Dunford'
'Kathleen Wheeler'
'Keith Richardson'
'Kiri Te Kanawa'
'Lady Caroline Nevill'
'Lady Londesborough'

'Lady Northcliffe'
'Lasurstern'
'Liberation'
'Lincoln Star'
'Lord Nevill'
'Louise Rowe'
'Marcel Moser'
'Marie Boisselot'
'Masquerade' (syn.
     'Maskarad')
'Maureen'
'Miss Bateman'
'Miss Crawshay'
'Monte Cassino'
'Moonlight'
'Mrs. Bush'
'Mrs. Cholmondeley'
'Mrs. George Jackman'
'Mrs. Hope'
'Mrs. James Mason'
'Mrs. N. Thompson'
'Mrs. P. B. Truax'
'Mrs. Spencer Castle'
'Multi Blue'
'Myôjô'
'Nelly Moser'
'Niobe'
'Peveril Pearl'
'Pink Fantasy'

'Pôhjanael'
'Prins Hendrik'
'Proteus'
'Ramona'
'Richard Pennell'
'Rouge Cardinal'
'Royal Velvet'
'Royalty'
'Ruby Glow'
'Scartho Gem'
'Sealand Gem'
'Serenata'
'Silver Moon'
'Snow Queen'
'Sugar Candy'
'Sunset'
'Sylvia Denny'
'The President'
'The Vagabond'
'Twilight'
'Wada's Primrose'
'Warszawaska Nike'
'W. E. Gladstone'
'Will Goodwin'
'William Kennett'
'Victoria'
'Vino'
'Violet Elizabeth'
'Vyvyan Pennell'

CLEMATIS IN PRUNING GROUP 3

Clematis addisonii
Clematis aethusifolia
Clematis × aromatica
Clematis × bonstedtii
    'Crépuscule'
Clematis campaniflora
Clematis crispa
Clematis × durandii
Clematis × eriostemon
Clematis flammula
Clematis fusca var.
    violacea
Clematis heracleifolia
    var. *davidiana*
    'Wyevale'
Clematis hirsutissima
Clematis integrifolia
    'Alba'
    'Rosea'
Clematis × jouiniana
    'Praecox'

Clematis ladakhiana
Clematis potaninii
Clematis recta
    'Purpurea'
Clematis rehderiana
Clematis serratifolia
Clematis tangutica
Clematis terniflora
Clematis texensis
Clematis tibetana
Clematis × triternata
    'Rubromarginata'
Clematis viticella
    'Mary Rose'
    'Purpurea Plena
    Elegans'
'Abundance'
'Alba Luxurians'
'Arabella'
'Ascotiensis'
'Betty Corning'

'Bill MacKenzie'
'Black Prince'
'Blue Angel' (syn.
    'Blekitny Aniol')
'Blue Boy'
'Comtesse de
    Bouchaud'
'Duchess of Albany'
'Dorothy Walton'
'Elvan'
'Ernest Markham'
'Etoile Rose'
'Etoile Violette'
'Gipsy Queen'
'Gravetye Beauty'
'Guiding Star'
'Hagley Hybrid'
'Huldine'
'Jackmanii'
'Jackmanii Superba'
'John Huxtable'
'Kermesina'
'Lady Betty Balfour'

'Lady Bird Johnson'
'Madame Edouard
    André'
'Madame Julia
    Correvon'
'Madame Grangé'
'Margaret Hunt'
'Margot Koster'
'Minuet'
'Pagoda'
'Paul Farges'
'Perle d'Azur'
'Perrin's Pride'
'Pink Fantasy'
'Polish Spirit'
'Prince Charles'
'Princess Diana'
'Rhapsody'
'Rouge Cardinal'
'Royal Velours'
'Venosa Violacea'
'Victoria'
'Ville de Lyon'

PRUNING GROUP 3

This group consists of all the species and large-flowered clematis that bloom from mid- to late summer, in which the stems grow and bloom in the same season. Many, including herbaceous types and texensis, die back during winter. They can all be hard-pruned in late winter or early spring every year, cutting back all stems to within 12in/30cm of the ground. Prune as growth starts so that you can cut stems back to good buds.

1 **Remove** any dead growth (on which buds are not visibly breaking). Be careful not to damage any new shoots coming from the base.

2 **Cut back** the remaining stems just above a pair of healthy buds 6–12in/15–30cm above ground level. Make a straight cut across the stem.

HOW TO PRUNE TO PROLONG FLOWERING

It is possible to extend the flowering season of clematis in Pruning Group 3, such as the viticellas, and a few of those in Pruning Group 2, such as large-flowered 'Niobe', by additional pruning during the growing season. Once the young shoots have grown to 12–20in/30–50cm long in early summer, prune half of them back to encourage more new shoots that will bear their flowers later than the first. Remember that many Group 2 large-flowered hybrids produce a few blooms later in the summer anyway, so this technique is worth trying only for those that do not have a second flush.

▶ EXTENDING FLOWERING ON A VITICELLA
Regular pruning reduces the shoots to within 12in/30cm of the ground. In early summer, prune half back again, cutting to just above a node.

BEFORE EXTRA PRUNING   AFTER EXTRA PRUNING

PROPAGATING YOUR OWN PLANTS

C LEMATIS CAN BE PROPAGATED from cuttings or seed, or by layering. Taking cuttings is the most popular method and produces plants identical to their parent. Named cultivars or hybrids, such as 'Nelly Moser', can be reproduced only from cuttings or by layering. Sowing seed from any of the species usually produces offspring that are the same, but from other clematis it is impossible to be sure what characteristics the new plants will have – which can lead to exciting results.

TAKING CUTTINGS

For a first attempt at taking cuttings, choose a clematis that roots readily, such as one of the montanas or *Clematis tibetana*. There are several methods, but taking internodal

cuttings (*below*) is the most reliable. A node is the joint between a leaf or leaves and the stem, so taking an internodal cutting means severing the stem in between pairs of leaves.

WHICH CLEMATIS

EASY TO ROOT
Alpinas
Montanas
Clematis tangutica
Clematis tibetana
'Bill MacKenzie'

MODERATELY EASY
Macropetalas
Viticellas
Large-flowered hybrids

DIFFICULT TO ROOT
Clematis armandii
Texensis

CHOOSING MATERIAL
Cuttings are best taken in early summer from new stems. Cut a growing shoot and select the best cuttings from it. Several cuttings can be made from a length of new growth, using all but the soft tip and hard, woody stem at the base.

Growth too soft

4 cuttings can be taken from the central portion of this stem, one for each pair of leaves

Growth too hard

1 **Make the first cut** on the main stem between 2 leaf joints (nodes), about 1½–2in/ 4–5cm below the top node, using a sharp knife or craft knife (preferably with a fresh blade).

2 **Make the second cut** just barely above the node. To make the operation safer, press the knife against a hard, clean surface as you cut.

3 **Trim off the leaves** on one side of the stem to lessen the effects of transpiration (water loss through leaves). This may not be necessary for clematis with very small or fine leaves.

4 **Unless the leaves are** very small, cut away one leaflet and its stalk. Always leave at least 2 leaflets to sustain the cutting through its rooting period.

Make sure cutting is correctly labeled

5 **Dip the stem base** in hormone rooting powder. Insert into a pot or tray filled with a mixture of peat, sharp sand, and perlite (*see Practical Tips, below*). Water in.

6 **Label and date** the cuttings and place in good light out of direct sun in a closed case or cover the pot with a plastic bag. Rooting should occur after about 6 weeks.

POTTING UP A ROOTED CUTTING

When the roots have developed and start to show at the base of the pot, pot the cuttings individually into 3½in/9cm pots using general potting mix. Water well and place in a cold frame or sheltered spot. Keep out of direct sun for the first 7–10 days. Check regularly and, when the roots fill this pot, repot into a 2-quart/2-liter pot. Grow on for a year before planting out.

Roots should be reasonably well developed before potting

PRACTICAL TIPS

• Use a soil mix consisting of 50 percent peat, 25 percent sharp sand, and 25 percent perlite.
• Cuttings taken in early summer root fastest.
• Heat at the base of the container will encourage the cuttings to root quicker.
• Keep cuttings clean and remove rotting leaves to prevent mold.
• Plants grown from cuttings should flower in 2 years.

SOWING SEED

Growing clematis from seed can be exciting: there is always a chance of getting a new or improved flower. Hybrids and cultivars do not come true from seed, nor will the species if they have been cross-pollinated by other clematis in your own or a neighbor's garden. To collect seed, pinch off the fluffy seedheads when they are just turning from green to brown in the autumn. They can be cold-stored, dried, or sown immediately. Plants grown from seed generally take longer to flower than those grown from cuttings or layers.

TYPES TO GROW FROM SEED

Clematis alpina	Clematis napaulensis
Clematis campaniflora	Clematis orientalis
Clematis chiisanensis	Clematis pitcheri
Clematis chrysochoma	Clematis recta
Clematis crispa	Clematis rehderiana
Clematis flammula	Clematis serratifolia
Clematis fusca	Clematis tangutica
Clematis integrifolia	Clematis terniflora
Clematis japonica	Clematis viorna
Clematis koreana	Clematis virginiana
Clematis macropetala	Clematis viticella
Clematis montana	

1 **To collect seed,** pick off the seedheads from the plant. Separate the fluffy strands. You can pinch off the tails, but be sure to keep the swollen base, which contains the seed.

2 **Holding the seeds** between your thumb and forefinger, spread them evenly across a gritty seed mix. Water in well and cover with a layer of grit or sharp sand.

3 **Label each pot** and place in a cold frame, plunging the pots, if possible, into sand to maintain an even temperature and moisture. Seedlings may take two years to emerge.

4 **Prick out the seedlings** when large enough to handle (with at least 4 leaves). Use a tool to remove them and hold them by the lowest leaves, not the fragile stem.

The seedling needs lots of light to make good growth

Make sure that the pot is labeled

5 **Plant each seedling** into a 3½in/9cm pot filled with potting mix; firm in gently. Water in, label, and grow on under glass, providing shade for the first 10 days.

GROWING ON
Initial shade helps the seedling's roots re-establish. Then it needs good light, preferably in a greenhouse. When the roots fill the pot, transfer to a 2–quart/ 2–liter pot and grow on before planting out.

LAYERING

Bury a stem from the parent plant in the ground or in a pot filled with potting mix, making a notch to induce roots to grow. Wait 1–2 years for good roots to develop (the shoot will offer strong resistance if gently tugged), then sever the new plant from its parent and pot up or plant out.

BEST TYPES FOR LAYERING

Alpinas, macropetalas, montanas, viticellas, large-flowered hybrids, *Clematis armandii*, *Clematis campaniflora*, *Clematis cirrhosa*, *Clematis florida*, *Clematis terniflora*, *Clematis texensis*, *Clematis tibetana*, *Clematis tangutica*, *Clematis serratifolia*

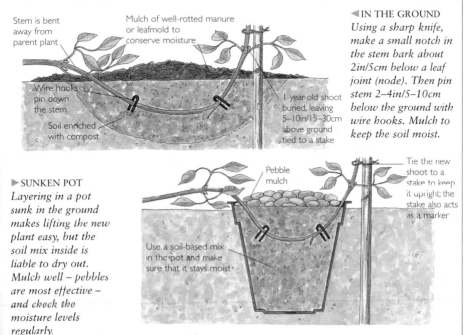

Stem is bent away from parent plant

Mulch of well-rotted manure or leafmold to conserve moisture

Wire hooks pin down the stem

Soil enriched with compost

1-year-old shoot buried, leaving 5–10in/15–30cm above ground tied to a stake

◄ IN THE GROUND
Using a sharp knife, make a small notch in the stem bark about 2in/5cm below a leaf joint (node). Then pin stem 2–4in/5–10cm below the ground with wire hooks. Mulch to keep the soil moist.

► SUNKEN POT
Layering in a pot sunk in the ground makes lifting the new plant easy, but the soil mix inside is liable to dry out. Mulch well – pebbles are most effective – and check the moisture levels regularly.

Pebble mulch

Use a soil-based mix in the pot and make sure that it stays moist

Tie the new shoot to a stake to keep it upright; the stake also acts as a marker

A GALLERY OF CLEMATIS

Arranged according to flowering time, this gallery begins with species that bloom in late winter and early spring, progressing through the spring-flowering clematis to the large-flowered hybrids of summer, and closing with the species that bloom in autumn. Hardiness zones are given as Z x–x.

EARLY-FLOWERING SPECIES

THE WINTER AND EARLY SPRING-FLOWERING SPECIES grow and bloom best in milder areas where the buds are less prone to cold damage; both *Clematis armandii* and *C. cirrhosa* benefit from the protection of a sheltered wall. Little pruning is necessary since all these clematis are in Pruning Group 1 (*see p.40*).

Clematis armandii   Z 7–9
Evergreen, with almond-scented flowers. To 20ft/6m.

Clematis cirrhosa   Z 7–9
Evergreen; may flower all winter. To 10–13ft/3–4m.

Clematis koreana   Z 7–9
Spring flowers from deep red to yellow. To 10–13ft/3–4m.

MORE CHOICES

Clematis armandii 'Apple Blossom' Pink buds
Clematis cirrhosa var. *balearica* Ferny foliage
Clematis cirrhosa 'Freckles' Maroon-spotted flowers

***Clematis* 'Pruinina'**   Z 6–8
Seedheads follow the splayed bells. To 6–10ft/2–3m.

Clematis indivisa   Z 7–9
Fragrant evergreen, best grown under glass. To 10–13ft/3–4m.

SHADES OF BLUE *The hybrid 'Mrs. Cholmondeley' flowers from late spring through summer.*

ALPINAS AND MACROPETALAS

THE SMALL NODDING FLOWERS of these clematis start to open in early spring – those of the alpinas are single, while those of the macropetalas are semidouble. Fluffy seedheads follow the flowers. Both kinds are quite hardy (Zones 6–9) and can be planted against north and east walls, where they will reach 6–13ft/2–4m. They also look attractive trained to climb into small trees or allowed to scramble through shrubs (*see p.20*). Little pruning is needed since all belong to Pruning Group 1 (*see p.40*), but they can be cut back immediately after flowering if necessary.

Clematis alpina 'Rosy Pagoda'
Pink bells. To 10–13ft/3–4m.

Clematis alpina 'Columbine'
Of the blue alpina cultivars, this is the closest to the wild species. To 6–10ft/2–3m.

Clematis alpina 'Willy'
Pale, mauve-pink flowers; sometimes has a second flush in summer. To 13ft/4m.

Clematis alpina 'Helsingborg'
Unusual purple; among the darkest alpinas. To 10ft/3m.

Clematis alpina 'Ruby'
Subtle, dusky red blooms. Vigorous, with good repeat flowering. To 10–13ft/3–4m.

Clematis alpina 'Tage Lundell'
Looks good against a pale backdrop. To 10ft/3m.

Clematis alpina 'Frances Rivis'
The blue petals are extra long and twisting. To 13ft/4m.

Clematis macropetala
'Maidwell Hall'
Fluffy seedheads follow the
blue flowers. To 8ft/2.5m.

'Rosie O'Grady'
Canadian-bred hybrid with
large flowers in a delicate
shade of pink. To 10ft/3m.

Clematis macropetala
'Markham's Pink'
Grows to 10ft/3m; produces
masses of lantern flowers.

Clematis macropetala
Very tough; it thrives in most
locations. Seedheads last
several months. To 11ft/3.5m.

'White Swan'
A fairly compact plant that
does not start flowering until
late spring. To 6ft/2m.

MORE CHOICES

Clematis alpina
   'Constance' Rich purple-
   pink flowers
   'Frankie' Mid-blue
   'Pink Flamingo' Pale pink
   subsp. *sibirica* 'White
   Moth' Pure white
Clematis macropetala
   'Lagoon'
   (syn. 'Blue Lagoon')
   Deep blue

THE MONTANAS

Clematis montana
'Elizabeth'
Vanilla scent; to 30ft/10m.

INTRODUCED FROM THE HIMALAYAS in 1831, *Clematis montana* has become one of the most popular of all clematis, particularly for covering walls and fences. The montanas are vigorous, reaching 20–30ft/6–10m or even more. The wild species has white flowers about 2in/5cm across, but it has given rise to many other forms, some with pink and purple-pink petals, often with bronze-tinted young foliage. Flowering time is from late spring to early summer. They need little or no pruning (*see Pruning Group 1, p.40*) and flower best in full sun. Hardiness zones 6–9.

Clematis montana
'Fragrant Spring'
Scented flowers; young leaves tinged purple. To 30ft/10m.

Clematis montana
'Tetrarose'
Large scented flowers; bronze-green leaves; to 25ft/8m.

Clematis montana var.
sericea
Best flower form; lacks scent. To 25ft/8m. Syn. 'Spooneri'.

Clematis montana var.
rubens
Very hardy; a little variable in
color. Climbs to 25ft/8m.

Clematis montana
The wild species has scented,
white flowers; ideal growing
through trees. To 40ft/12m.

Clematis montana
'Warwickshire Rose'
Most vigorous of the bronze-
leaved forms. To 30ft/10m.

Clematis montana
f. *grandiflora*
Blooms up to 3in/8cm wide;
grows to 35ft/11m.

Clematis chrysocoma
Less rampant, reaching about
6ft/2m; related to *C. montana*
but with rounder leaves.

MORE CHOICES

Clematis montana
  'Broughton Star' Creamy
    pink, semidouble
  'Freda' Pink with
    bronze foliage
  'Marjorie' Pink, semi-
    double
  'Mayleen' Scented pink
    flowers, bronze foliage
  'Picton's Variety' Deep
    pink flowers with
    bronze foliage
var. *wilsonii* White

EARLY LARGE-FLOWERED HYBRIDS

Clematis patens
Used in breeding many in this group. To about 6ft/2m.

THE INTRODUCTION FROM JAPAN in 1836 of *Clematis patens*, and later of *C. lanuginosa* and *C. florida* from China, gave rise to an enormous number of large-flowered hybrids. This group has been divided over the following pages according to color and includes midseason types, with a separate section for double-flowered hybrids. Most of these clematis flower in late spring and early summer, with many producing a repeat flush of flowers in late summer. All require light pruning (*see Pruning Group 2, pp.41–42*). Hardiness zones 4–9.

'Lady Londesborough'
Bred in 1869 and resembles *C. patens*; flowering season is rather short. To 6ft/2m.

'Mrs. Cholmondeley'
A clematis that will flower all summer with light pruning. It will climb to 10–13ft/3–4m.

'William Kennett'
Free-flowering, with blooms 7in/18cm across. Easy to grow and vigorous; to 10ft/3m.

'Richard Pennell'
Prominent stamens and undulating petals with rosy pink shading. To 10ft/3m.

'Lady Northcliffe'
A popular clematis for its long flowering season and deep blue blooms. To 6ft/2m.

'Elsa Späth'
Easy to grow and flowers well from mid- to late season. Reaches 8–10ft/2.5–3m.

'Blue Ravine'
This is a reliable new clematis that has petals marked with strong veining. To 10ft/3m.

'The President'
In flower nearly all summer, this is an old favorite from 1876. To 10–13ft/3–4m.

'Lasurstern'
The plant becomes smothered in flowers, with a few blooms later in the year. To 10ft/3m.

'Mrs. Hope'
Large flowers up to 6in/15cm across with striking deep red anthers. Climbs to 12ft/3.5m.

'Ramona'
Large blooms with a deep red center. Flowers best in full sun; grows to 10–13ft/3–4m.

'H. F. Young'
Nearly perfect blue flowers with a contrasting eye of cream stamens. To 8ft/2.5m.

'W. E. Gladstone'
Flowers lightly over a long time; huge blooms up to 10in/ 25cm across. To 12ft/3.5m.

MORE CHOICES

'Beauty of Richmond' Pale mauve
'Général Sikorski' Very lovely blue
'Haku-ôkan' Violet
'Joan Picton' A mass of pinkish mauve flowers
'Kathleen Wheeler' Blue with purple midribs
'Lady Caroline Nevill' Soft blue
'Mrs. P. B. Truax' Pale blue
'North Star' (syn. 'Pôhjanael') Deep blue

'John Warren'
Large flowers up to 7in/18cm in diameter; dark pink edges to pointed petals. To 10ft/3m.

'Lincoln Star'
A strong, reliable variety that flowers prolifically over its entire height of about 10ft/3m.

'Charissima'
This clematis has lovely large, pale flowers with complex cerise veining. To 8ft/2.5m.

'Dr. Ruppel'
A striking, deep rose color that is not for the faint-hearted. To about 10ft/3m.

'Mrs. N. Thompson'
A compact clematis, reaching 6ft/2m, with blue-purple flowers with a deep pink bar.

'The Vagabond'
The rich purple and crimson of the velvety petals offsets the cream stamens. To 8ft/2.5m.

'Carnaby'
An ideal container clematis,
growing to 8ft/2.5m; flowers
of a glowing deep pink.

'Fireworks'
More vigorous than 'Mrs. N.
Thompson'; its flowers live up
to its name. To 10ft/3m.

'Nelly Moser'
The flowers of this popular
clematis keep their color best
in shade. To about 10ft/3m.

'Bees' Jubilee'
A compact clematis, growing
to only 6ft/2m and therefore
ideal for containers.

MORE STRIPED-FLOWERED CHOICES

'Andromeda' Semidouble
pale pink with darker stripe
'Asao' Deep pink with paler
midribs
'Barbara Jackman' Deep
purple-blue with
contrasting magenta bar
'Carnival Queen' Pink with
deep cerise edges
'Etoile de Malicorne' Mauve
with red-purple bar
'Fair Rosamond' Pale blush
pink with deeper bar that
fades; some fragrance

'John Paul II' (syn. 'Jan
Pawel II') Pale pink with
darker stripe
'Keith Richardson' Purple-red
with paler midribs
'Masquerade' (syn.
'Maskarad') Pale pink with
deeper-colored bar
'Mrs. James Mason' Violet-
blue with deep red bar
'Pink Fantasy' Small pink
with darker bar
'Sealand Gem' Lavender-blue
with dark pink bar

'Miss Bateman'
Produces a single but profuse flowering. A compact clematis, reaching about 6ft/2m.

'Snow Queen'
Flowers well even when young and has lovely, wavy-edged blooms. Grows to 8ft/2.5m.

'Barbara Dibley'
Flowers well in sun but retains color intensity best in light shade. Can reach 10ft/3m.

'Guernsey Cream'
Blooms prolifically and is one of the earliest hybrids of all to flower. Climbs to 8ft/2.5m.

'Vino'
Produces the finest show of its vibrant flowers if grown in full sun. Climbs to 10ft/3m.

'Gillian Blades'
A compact grower and one of the best of the early white-flowered hybrids. To 8ft/2.5m.

'Marie Boisselot'
Flowers tend to be produced
high up on this clematis,
which can reach 12ft/3.5m.

'Jackmanii Rubra'
Free-flowering; first blooms
may be semidouble (*see* Mrs.
G. Jackman, *p.61*). To 10ft/3m.

'Moonlight'
Provides light cover; the
delicate flower coloring is best
in shade. Grows to 8ft/2.5m.

'Henryi'
A classic clematis, bred as
early as 1858 and deservedly
still popular. To 12ft/3.5m.

'Niobe'
A few stems can be hard-
pruned to extend its flowering
season. Grows to 10ft/3m.

MORE CHOICES

'Corona' Pinkish red

'Crimson King' Dark red

'Cardinal Wyszinski' (syn
 'Kardynal Wyszyñski')
 Purple-red

'Maureen' Violet-purple
 with red midribs

'Monte Cassino' Velvety
 red-purple

'Edith' A short-growing
 white

'James Mason' White with
 dark stamens

'Silver Moon' Silver-gray

EARLY DOUBLE HYBRIDS

THE SHOWY FLOWERS produced by these clematis appeared originally on sports of large-flowered hybrids. (Sports are natural mutations that exhibit differences from the norm.) Double flowers occur only in the early-flowered hybrids and usually just on the first flowers in early summer; any subsequent flowers are single. Some hybrids have just two rows of sepals; these are known as "semidouble." Early double hybrids require light pruning (*see Pruning Group 2, pp.41–42*); pruning too hard results in later, single flowers. Hardiness zones 4–9.

'Kathleen Dunford'
Semidouble, so the stamens still stand out. To 8ft/2.5m.

'Multi Blue'
The unusually formed flowers of this clematis are long-lasting. Grows to 8ft/2.5m.

'Belle of Woking'
A good grower, up to 8ft/2.5m, with a few flowers later in the year that may also be double.

'Vyvyan Pennell'
One of the best-known doubles, with velvety-textured flowers. To 8–10ft/2.5–3m.

'Duchess of Edinburgh'
After cold weather, the flowers can be quite green when they first open. To 8ft/2.5m.

'Mrs. George Jackman'
A semidouble that has a longer season when planted in light shade. Up to 8ft/2.5m.

'Countess of Lovelace'
This has more regularly spaced petals than most doubles. Grows to 8ft/2.5m.

'Proteus'
The flowers look best against a variegated or golden-leaved shrub. Grows to 8ft/2.5m.

'Royalty'
A deep violet that contrasts well with soft yellow flowers or foliage. To about 6ft/2m.

MORE CHOICES

'Arctic Queen' Pure white
'Beauty of Worcester' Mid-blue
'Chalcedony' Pale blue
'Kiri Te Kanawa' Deep blue
'Miss Crawshay' Pinkish mauve, semidouble
'Mrs. Spencer Castle' Mauve-pink, semidouble
'Sylvia Denny' White, semidouble
'Violet Elizabeth' Mauve-pink

LATE LARGE-FLOWERED HYBRIDS

THE EXUBERANT FLOWERS of these clematis enliven any garden in late summer and early autumn. Large-flowered hybrids are best given the support of a climbing rose or other shrub, so that excessive training of the shoots is not so necessary. They look superb when allowed to twine in and out of roses, buddleias, and other late-summer shrubs. Like all clematis that flower after midsummer, these belong to Pruning Group 3 (*see pp.42–43*) and should be cut back to within 12in/30cm of the ground in late winter or early spring. Hardiness zones 4–9.

'Hagley Hybrid'
The subtle color is suited to planting in shade. To 8ft/2.5m.

'Huldine'
The upward-facing flowers are at their best toward the end of summer. To 16–20ft/5–6m.

'Ernest Markham'
A tall clematis, up to 13ft/4m, with vivid magenta blooms. It does well in full sun.

'Ville de Lyon'
Flowers freely, especially if lightly pruned rather than cut back hard. Grows to 10ft/3m.

'Comtesse de Bouchaud'
Old, reliable variety that has masses of vibrant, mauve-pink blooms. To 10ft/3m.

'Ascotiensis'
A strong-growing cultivar, reaching about 10ft/3m, with a very long flowering season.

'Jackmanii'
The most popular variety for cottage gardens, with velvety, purple flowers. To 10ft/3m.

'Rouge Cardinal'
The deep crimson blooms
have an especially rich,
velvety texture. To 10ft/3m.

'Victoria'
A vigorous clematis that
grows well in cold climates,
reaching about 10–13ft/3–4m.

'Prince Charles'
A reliable, long-flowering,
and compact hybrid, seldom
reaching more than 6ft/2m.

MORE CHOICES

'Blue Angel' (syn. 'Blekitny
   Aniol') Pale blue
'Dorothy Walton' Lilac
'Guiding Star' Violet-purple
   with plum bar
'John Huxtable' White
'Lady Betty Balfour'
   Purple-blue
'Margaret Hunt' Lilac
'Madame Edouard André'
   Deep red
'Perle d'Azur' Sky blue
'Perrin's Pride' Purple
'Rhapsody' Electric blue

'Gipsy Queen'
The tapering bases of the
petals make the flowers stand
out well. Grows to 10ft/3m.

'Madame Grangé'
Vigorous and free flowering,
petals are gray and woolly on
the reverse. To 10ft/3m.

HERBACEOUS CLEMATIS

Clematis × aromatica Z 4–8
A hybrid with fragrant flowers
on a mound 3–6ft/1–2m high.

THESE CLEMATIS DO NOT TWINE. They vary from types such as *Clematis heracleifolia* that can be grown as a self-supporting groundcover, to those such as *C. integrifolia* and *C. recta* that tend to lean on other plants. All are attractive in mixed plantings. Support floppy types with stakes or plant rings, or allow them to hang over retaining walls or sprawl at the front of borders. Herbaceous clematis usually have much smaller flowers than other types, sometimes fragrant. As for most herbaceous plants, prune hard in late winter (*see Pruning Group 3, pp.42–43*).

Clematis × bonstedtii
'Crépuscule' Z 6–8
Tiny, tubelike flowers have a
sweet fragrance; to 3ft/1m.

Clematis integrifolia Z 3–7
Sepals have a pronounced
twist. Plants barely reach
3ft/1m in height.

Clematis × jouiniana
'Praecox' Z 4–9
Makes a vigorous groundcover,
scrambling for 13–16ft/4–5m.

Clematis recta
'Purpurea' Z 3–7
Purplish gray young foliage;
white flowers. To 5ft/1.5m.

Clematis recta Z 3–7
This species reaches 5ft/1.5m
but tends to flop; it mixes
well in herbaceous plantings.

Clematis integrifolia
'Rosea' Z 3–7
Has larger flowers than the
species (*opposite*). To 3ft/1m.

Clematis x *durandii* Z 6–9
Long-flowering and superb
for growing through a small
shrub. To about 5ft/1.5m.

Clematis heracleifolia var.
davidiana 'Wyevale' Z 3–8
Bold foliage and fragrant
flowers. Up to 3ft/1m.

MORE CHOICES

Clematis heracleifolia var.
  davidiana Very fragrant
Clematis hirsutissima
  Needs dry alpine
  conditions
Clematis integrifolia '**Alba**'
  White form of the species
  (*opposite*)
Clematis songarica Sturdy,
  almost shrublike species
  with white flowers
'**Arabella**' Small blue
  flowers all summer

VITICELLAS AND TEXENSIS

THE "VIRGIN'S BOWER" – *Clematis viticella* – is a native of Europe and has been known in gardens since 1569. It has small, purple, bell-like flowers in late summer and has been much used in hybridizing. *Clematis texensis*, a species from the US with scarlet, urn-shaped flowers, is responsible for the red tones in all red hybrids. Viticella and texensis cultivars and hybrids are easy to grow and particularly suitable for combining with shrubs. They grow 6–16ft/2–5m tall and need hard pruning (*see Pruning Group 3, pp.42–3*). Hardiness: viticellas Z5–9, texensis Z4–9.

'Minuet'
Starry flowers with mauve markings on white. To 10ft/3m.

Clematis viticella 'Purpurea Plena Elegans'
The double flowers last for several weeks. To 10ft/3m.

'Madame Julia Correvon'
Prolific and long-flowering, with larger blooms than most viticellas. Grows to 12ft/3.5m.

'Venosa Violacea'
Uniquely patterned flowers show up well against plants with silver foliage. To 10ft/3m.

'Etoile Violette'
Masses of dark flowers that look best offset by a pale-leaved plant. To 13ft/4m.

'Abundance'
Profuse flowering and the best pinkish red clematis in this group. Grows to 10ft/3m.

'Pagoda'
A superb clematis with deeply reflexed petals with a grayish-pink reverse. Grows to 6ft/2m.

'Kermesina'
The intense crimson blooms
look stunning in sunlight.
Generally to about 10ft/3m.

'Alba Luxurians'
White flowers with a dark
eye; the first flush has green
markings. Grows to 10ft/3m.

'Betty Corning'
American-bred with reflexed
flowers that have a slight
fragrance. Grows to 8ft/2.5m.

'Duchess of Albany'
The pretty, pink, tulip-shaped
flowers stand up well above
small shrubs. To 10ft/3m.

'Gravetye Beauty'
The deepest red flowers but
the weakest growing of the
texensis; can grow to 10ft/3m.

Clematis texensis
The species, up to 10ft/3m, is
rare in cultivation but has been
much used in hybridizing.

'Lady Bird Johnson'
Lovely pitcher-shaped flowers
with petals with a contrasting,
pale reverse. To 6–10ft/2–3m.

'Etoile Rose'
Needs a tall support to
display the bells well; flowers
for 3 months. To 8ft/2.5m.

MORE CHOICES

Clematis viticella
  'Mary Rose' Double
    smoky purple
'Black Prince' Purple
'Elvan' Small blue-purple
'Margot Koster' Deep
    rosy pink
'Polish Spirit' Rich
    purple-blue
'Princess Diana' Deep
    cherry pink
'Royal Velours' Rich
    purple-red

MID- TO LATE-FLOWERING SPECIES

S OME OF THE MOST INTERESTING CLEMATIS are
included in this group. Apart from *Clematis
florida*, a parent of many of the large-flowered
hybrids, they are mostly small-flowered and bloom
from midsummer onward. All except *C. florida*
require hard pruning (*see Pruning Group 3,
pp.42–43*). *Clematis tibetana* (*see p.26*) and
C. tangutica are familiar for their thick-sepaled
yellow bells and fluffy seedheads, while others, such
as *C. terniflora* and *C. rehderiana*, carry bunches
of small, fragrant stars or bells.

Clematis florida
'Sieboldii'   Z 6–9
Exotic-looking; to 10ft/3m.

'Paul Farges'   Z 6–8
A vigorous hybrid that flowers
reliably for 2–3 months and
can reach 20–25ft/6–8m.

Clematis rehderiana Z 6–9
Late summer flowers with a
sweet fragrance. This clematis
can reach up to 20ft/6m.

Clematis serratifolia Z 6–8
Pale bells are followed by
fluffy seedheads; grows up to
about 15ft/5m.

Clematis x *triternata*
'Rubromarginata'   Z 6–9
A reliable hybrid with clouds
of scented flowers; to 15ft/5m.

Clematis flammula   Z 7–9
A Mediterranean species with
clouds of small, fragrant
flowers; grows up to 15ft/5m.

Clematis campaniflora Z 7–9
A species from Portugal with
very small, dainty bells; it can
climb to 15ft/5m.

Clematis tangutica   Z 6–9
Carries flowers and fluffy
seedheads at the same time;
grows up to about 15ft/5m.

'Bill MacKenzie'   Z 6–9
Possibly the best yellow
autumn clematis for flowers
and seedheads; up to 23ft/7m.

Clematis x eriostemon Z 4–9
A semiherbaceous hybrid that
flowers for 3 months.
It grows to 8ft/2.5m.

Clematis ladakhiana Z 6–9
A curiously colored species
from the Himalayas, reaching
to 15ft/5m; needs full sun.

C. ladakhiana (seedhead)
The seedheads of this species
and the *Clematis tibetana*
types close the clematis year.

MORE CHOICES

Clematis aethusifolia
Parsleylike leaves and
creamy bells
Clematis crispa Pale blue
bells
Clematis florida 'Flore Pleno'
Double green and white
Clematis fusca var. *violacea*
Hairy purple-brown bells
Clematis terniflora Profuse,
fragrant white stars
Clematis tibetana (syn.
C. orientalis 'Sherriffii')
Yellow bells and grayish
foliage

INDEX

Page numbers in *italics* indicate illustrations. Species and hybrids are listed under the first letter of their name rather than C for clematis.

A
'Abundance' 66, *66*
addisonii 35, *35*
aethusifolia 11
akebioides 11
'Alba Luxurians' 12, 67, *67*
alpina 50–51
colors 13
in containers 25
flower shape 7, 10
propagation 44, 46, 47
pruning 38
seedheads 11
supports 16, 20, 21, 23
a. 'Columbine' 50, *50*
a. 'Frances Rivis' 13, 50, *50*
a. 'Helsingborg' 50, *50*
a. 'Rosy Pagoda' 10, 50, *50*
a. 'Ruby' 50, *50*
a. 'Tage Lundell' 50, *50*
a. 'White Moth' 12
a. 'Willy' 13, 50, *50*
aphids 34
'Arabella' 25
armandii 7, 10, *10*, 12, *12*, 22, *22*, 38, 44, 49, *49*
a. 'Apple Blossom' 22, *22*
× aromatica 64, *64*
'Asao' 15
'Ascotiensis' 62, *62*

B
'Barbara Dibley' 25, 58, *58*
barbellata 38
'Beauty of Worcester' 25
'Bees' Jubilee' 57, *57*
'Belle of Woking' 60, *60*
'Betty Corning' 67, *67*
'Bill MacKenzie' 9, 11, 13, 21, 38, *38*, 44, 69, *69*

'Blue Lagoon' 14
'Blue Ravine' 55, *55*
× bonstedtii 'Crépuscule' 64, *64*
border plantings 18–19

C
campaniflora 46, 47, 68, *68*
'Carnaby' 57, *57*
× cartmanii 'Joe' 25
'Charissima' 56, *56*
chiisanensis 46
chrysocoma 38, 46, 53, *53*
cirrhosa 10, 22, 38, 47, 49, *49*
c. var. balearica 11
colors 12–15
'Comtesse de Bouchaud' 6, *6*, 13, *13*, 24, *24*, 25, 62, *62*
containers 24–25
'Corona' 17
'Countess of Lovelace' 25, 61, *61*
crispa 16, 46
cuttings 44–45

D
'Dawn' 12
diseases 35
'Dr. Ruppel' 15, 56, *56*
double early-flowering hybrids 60–61
downspouts, attaching a trellis to 29
'Duchess of Albany' 15, 67, *67*
'Duchess of Edinburgh' 61, *61*
× durandii 15, 18, *18*, 65, *65*

E
earwigs 34
'Elsa Späth' 25, 54, *54*
× eriostemon 69, *69*
'Ernest Markham' 13, 15, 62, *62*

'Etoile Rose' 67, *67*
'Etoile Violette' 15, 23, *23*, 66, *66*

F
'Fireworks' 13, 21, *21*, 57, *57*
flammula 12, 19, *19*, 46, 68, *68*
florida 47
f. 'Flore Pleno' 25, 37, *37*
f. 'Sieboldii' 24, *24*, 68, *68*
flowering, prolonging 43
foliage 11
fungal infections 35
fusca 46

G
'Gillian Blades' 17, 58, *58*
'Gipsy Queen' 15, 63, *63*
globe, wire 36–7
gracilifolia 38
'Gravetye Beauty' 15, 67, *67*
'Guernsey Cream' 14, 58, *58*

H
'Hagley Hybrid' 17, *17*, 25, 62, *62*
'Henryi' 59, *59*
heracleifolia 11, 18
h. var. davidiana 19, *19*
h. var. davidiana 'Wyevale' 65, *65*
herbaceous clematis 18, 64–65
'H. F. Young' 25, 55, *55*
'Huldine' 12, 62, *62*
hybrids 54–63

I–J
indivisa 10, 49, *49*
integrifolia 15, 18, 46, 64, *64*
i. 'Rosea' 65, *65*
intricata 11
'Jackmanii' 8, 13, *13*, 62, *62*

Jackmanii group 11, 13, 19
'Jackmanii Rubra' 16, *16*,
    59, *59*
'James Mason' 12
japonica 46
'John Huxtable' 25
'John Warren' 13, *13*, 56, *56*
× *jouiniana* 18
    × *j*. 'Praecox' 64, *64*

K
'Kardynal Wyszynski' 20, *20*
'Kathleen Dunford' 60, *60*
'Kermesina' 8, *8*, 13, *67*, *67*
koreana 38, 46, 49, *49*

L
ladakhiana 11, 69, *69*
'Lady Bird Johnson' 67, *67*
'Lady Londesborough' 11,
    11, 54, *54*
'Lady Northcliffe' 13, 21, *21*,
    54, *54*
'Lasurstern' 55, *55*
layering 47
'Lincoln Star' 56, *56*

M
macropetala 50
    in containers 25
    flower shape 7, 10
    propagation 44, 46, 47
    pruning 38
    seedheads 11
    supports 16, 21, 23
    m. 'Maidwell Hall' 25, *25*,
        50
    m. 'Markham's Pink' 14,
        50
'Madame Grange' 63, *63*
'Madame Julia Correvon' 13,
    15, 66, *66*
'Margot Koster' 17
'Marie Boisselot' 12, *12*, 17,
    23, 59, *59*
mice 34
mildew 16, 35
'Minuet' 66, *66*

'Miss Bateman' 12, 25, 38,
    38, 58, *58*
'Miss Crawshay' 12
montana 11, 52–53
    colors 13, 14
    diseases 35
    flower shape 7
    propagation 44, 46, 47
    pruning 38
    supports 20, 21, 23
    m. 'Elizabeth' 52, *52*
    m. 'Fragrant Spring' 52, *52*
    m. f. *grandiflora* 12, 53, *53*
    m. var. *rubens* 53, *53*
    m. var. *sericea* 52, *52*
    m. 'Tetrarose' 13, 52, *52*
    m. 'Warwickshire Rose' 13,
        23, 53, *53*
'Moonlight' 59, *59*
'Mrs. Cholmondeley' 13, 17,
    17, 48, *48*, 54, *54*
'Mrs. George Jackman' 25,
    61, *61*
'Mrs. Hope' 55, *55*
'Mrs. N. Thompson' 56, *56*
'Multi Blue' 60, *60*

N–O
napaulensis 46
'Nelly Moser' 22, *22*, 44, 57,
    57
'Niobe' 12, *12*, 13, 25, 43,
    59, *59*
orientalis 11, 46 (*see also
    tibetana*)

P
'Pagoda' 66, *66*
paniculata see *terniflora*
patens 54, *54*
'Paul Farges' 21, 68, *68*
pegging down 33
'Perle d'Azur' 8, *8*, 13, 25
pests 34
pitcheri 46
planting 30–31
potaninii 12, 15, *15*, 21
'The President' 15, 22, *22*,
    55, *55*

'Prince Charles' 63, *63*
'Proteus' 25, 61, *61*
'Pruinina' 38, 49, *49*
pruning 38–43

R
'Ramona' 55, *55*
recta 9, *9*, 46, 65, *65*
    r. 'Purpurea' 11, 12, 18,
        65, *65*
rehderiana 12, *12*, 46, 68, *68*
renovating clematis 39
reticulata 35
'Richard Pennell' 54, *54*
roses, combining with 16–17
'Rosie O'Grady' 50
'Rouge Cardinal' 13, 63, *63*
'Royalty' 12, *12*, 14, 17, 61,
    61

S
seed, sowing 46–47
seedheads 11
serratifolia 13, 46, 68, *68*
shrubs, growing clematis in
    20–21, 31
'Silver Moon' 12, 17
slime flux 35
slugs 34
'Snow Queen' 58, *58*
songarica 46
sowing seed 46–47
supports 20–23, 28–29

T
tangutica 7, *9*, 69, *69*
    color 13
    propagation 44, 46, 47
    seedheads 11
    supports 21
terniflora 7, 9, 11, 12, 20
texensis 7, 11, 67, *67*
    in borders 19, 33
    diseases 16, 35
    propagation 44
tibetana 9, 11, *11*, 26, *26*,
    44, 47
    t. subsp. *vernayi* 11

training 32–33
trees, growing clematis in
    20–21
trellises 28–29
× *triternata* 'Rubromarginata'
    68, *68*
tying in 32

V

'The Vagabond' 12, *12*, 56, *56*
× *vedrariensis* 38
'Venosa Violacea' 66, *66*
'Victoria' 63, *63*
'Ville de Lyon' 13, 62, *62*

'Vino' 58, *58*
viorna 46
virginiana 46
vitalba 11
viticella 9, 11, 66
    in borders 15, 19, 33
    in containers 25
    flower shape 7
    propagation 44, 47
    pruning 43
    supports 16, 17
    v. 'Mary Rose' 14
    v. 'Purpurea Plena Elegans'
        66, *66*
'Vyvyan Pennell' 60, *60*

W–Z

'Wada's Primrose' 13
walls:
    attaching a trellis to
        28–29
    planting by 30
    watering 31
'W. E. Gladstone' 13, *13*,
    55, *55*
'White Swan' 14, 50
'William Kennett' 54, *54*
wilt 35

ACKNOWLEDGMENTS

Picture research Christine Rista

Special photography Richard Surman,
Peter Anderson

Illustrations Karen Cochrane

Index Hilary Bird

DK Publishing would like to thank:
All staff at the RHS, in particular Susanne
Mitchell, Karen Wilson and Barbara Haynes
at Vincent Square, also the team at the
propagation unit, Wisley; staff at Burford
House Gardens, Tenbury Wells,
Worcestershire; Agriframes Ltd (for supplying
the downspout trellis, p.29).

American Horticultural Society
Visit AHS at www.ahs.org or call them at
1-800-777-7931, ext. 10. Membership
benefits include *The American Gardener*
magazine, free admission to flower shows,
the free seed exchange, book services, and
the Gardener's Information Service.

Photography
The publisher would also like to thank the
following for their kind permission to
reproduce their photographs:
(key: t=top, c=center, b=below, l=left, r=right)

Mark Bolton: 54bl
Neil Campbell-Sharp: 20cr, 67tr
Charles Chesshire: 55cl
Eric Crichton Photos: jacket front tl, 4br, 7b,
8b, 8t, 9, 15tr, 15tl, 19br, 52bc, 56bl, 59tr,
65bl
DK Special Photography: Dave King 38bc
The Garden Picture Library: Howard Rice 2,
48; Jerry Pavia 26; John Glover 65tr, 67cc
John Glover: 24bl
Harpur Garden Library: 7c, 10r, 49cc
Andrew Lawson: 14, 17tr, 19tl, 20bl, 21br
Clive Nichols Garden Pictures: Pam
Schwert/S. Kreutzberger 24r
Photos Horticultural: 37br, 37bl 60bl, 61tr,
63bl, 63tl, 65tl, 69tr
Photo Lamontagne: 18
Harry Smith Collection: 25r, 25l, 37tr, 49br,
54cc, 63bc, 64tl, 64cr, 67cr, 67bl, 68bl, 69bc,
69bl
Richard Surman: 38br